CAREERS
EDUCATION
and
GUIDANCE

CAREERS EDUCATION and GUIDANCE

DAVID FROST · ANDREW EDWARDS
HELEN REYNOLDS

KOGAN PAGE

London ● Philadelphia

First published in 1995

Apart from any fair dealing for the purposes of research or private study, or criticism or review, as permitted under the Copyright, Designs and Patents Act, 1988, this publication may only be reproduced, stored or transmitted, in any form or by any means, with the prior permission in writing of the publishers, or in the case of reprographic reproduction in accordance with the terms of licences issued by the Copyright Licensing Agency. Enquiries concerning reproduction outside those terms should be sent to the publishers at the undermentioned address:

Kogan Page Limited
120 Pentonville Road
London, N1 9JN

© D Frost, A Edwards, H Reynolds, and named contributors, 1995.

British Library Cataloguing in Publication Data
A CIP record for this book is available from the British Library.
ISBN 0 7494 1728 5

Typeset by Kogan Page
Printed and bound in Great Britain by Biddles Ltd, Guildford and King's Lynn

CONTENTS

The Editors and Contributors   vii

Foreword   x

Introduction   1

Section One: The Context of Change

Chapter 1   Careers Education and Guidance in Schools: 6
Policy and Practice
AG Watts

Chapter 2   Careers Guidance and Careers Services: 12
Facing up to Change
Peter Heaviside

Chapter 3   What Governors and Managers Need to Know   19
Anthony Barnes

Section Two: Developing the Curriculum

Chapter 4   Careers Education and Guidance and the Action   28
Planning Process
Jacquie MacDonald

Chapter 5   Post-16 Careers Guidance: The Role of Tutorial   36
Methods in Supporting Good Practice
Andrew Edwards

Chapter 6   Careers Education and Guidance and Special   50
Educational Needs
Christine Thomas

Chapter 7   The Careers Education Curriculum: 55
The 'Education for Choice' Project
Andrew Edwards and Jean-Luc Mure with Greg Robb

Chapter 8   Using Computers in Careers Education and Guidance   67
             Marcus Offer
Chapter 9   Media Education and Careers Education and Guidance   74
             (or, I once saw a happy episode of *EastEnders*)
             Ken Fox

Section Three: Professional Development and Training

Chapter 10   Pilgrim's Progress: 84
             Encounters in Staff Development for Careers Work
             Bill Law
Chapter 11   Reflective Action Planning: A Model for Continuing   93
             Professional Development
             David Frost
Chapter 12   The Careers Work Training Partnership   105
             Helen Reynolds and David Frost
Chapter 13   Supporting Careers Advisers   109
             Jackie Hartley and Mike Shaw
Chapter 14   Case Studies in the Development of Careers   114
             Education
             Hilary Harber, Emma Hewitt and Gillian Bannister
Chapter 15   The Role of Careers Education in Social Renewal   131
             David Cleaton and Lesley Arnold

Section Four: Quality Assurance

Chapter 16   Quality and Standards in Careers Work   140
             Anthony Barnes
Chapter 17   Improving Professional Practice Through Evaluation   146
             David Frost

References and Further Reading   156

Glossary   160

Index   163

THE EDITORS AND CONTRIBUTORS

The Editors

David Frost is a Principal Lecturer in Education and has played a leading role in the development of continuing professional development programmes at Canterbury Christ Church College. He has made a significant contribution to the development of approaches to accreditation through portfolio development. He has previously published on mentoring, teacher education and pastoral care and his current research is concerned with the evaluation of school-based continuing professional development. David was instrumental in establishing partnerships between the college and a number of careers services.

Andrew Edwards is the Director of the Careers Work Centre, a specialist unit within the Education Department at Canterbury Christ Church College. Formerly, a secondary teacher and senior careers adviser, he latterly became the Development Manager for Kent Careers and Guidance Service. He has developed partnerships with academics and careers specialists in Canada, France and throughout the UK. His own research is in the field of curriculum and professional development and he is currently engaged in project management and consultancy work, together with piloting a new post-experience qualification for careers advisers.

Helen Reynolds is currently a Senior Lecturer in Education at Canterbury Christ Church College. After many years as a senior careers adviser, she concentrated on development work initially through the Technical and Vocational Education Initiative (TVEI), and later as a member of the Development Team with Kent Careers and Guidance Service. Helen's research interests focus on guidance and counselling. Within the Careers Work Centre, Helen is responsible for the coordination of accredited careers courses.

The Contributors

Lesley Arnold is Assistant Principal Careers Officer with East Sussex Careers Services. She has a particular interest in training and staff development and is an Associate Tutor with Canterbury Christ Church College.

Gillian Bannister is a senior teacher at Cannock Chase High School and responsible for Careers Education. She has recently completed the Careers Work Certificate course with Canterbury Christ Church College.

Anthony Barnes is President of the National Association of Careers Guidance Teachers (NACGT). He is a Curriculum and Training Consultant with Careers Enterprise Ltd, and formerly an Inspector with Surrey Education Authority and lead writer of the SCAA guidelines on CEG.

David Cleaton OBE is Head of East Sussex Careers Services and a well-established author and trainer in the field of careers education and guidance. He is an Associate Tutor with Canterbury Christ Church College.

Ken Fox is a Senior Lecturer in Media Education at Canterbury Christ Church College, and is author of 'Story to Story', a media education teaching pack for KS3 and KS4.

Hilary Harber is the Careers Coordinator at Oxted County School, Surrey and a recent participant in the Advanced Certificate in Careers Education and Guidance at Canterbury Christ Church College.

Jackie Hartley was the Guidance Development Manager for Staffordshire Careers Service at the time of writing. She is an experienced trainer in the careers field and an Associate Tutor for Canterbury Christ Church College. She is currently the Schools' Liaison Adviser at Newcastle-under-Lyme College.

Peter Heaviside is Chief Inspector of Careers Services and head of the Careers Service Quality Assurance and Development Unit, Department for Education and Employment.

Emma Hewitt is Careers Coordinator at Várndean Sixth Form College. She has recently completed the Careers Work Certificate course with Canterbury Christ Church College.

Bill Law is a Senior Fellow of the National Institute for Careers Education and Counselling (NICEC), principal author of *Careers Work*, published by the Open College, and a leading national figure in careers related research and development.

Jacquie MacDonald is a lecturer in Careers Education and Guidance at the University of London Institute of Education and an Advisory Teacher with the London Borough of Lambeth.

Jean-Luc Mure is Vice President of the Association Trouver Créer and Communications Manager for the Careers Service within the Académie de Grenoble.

Marcus Offer is a lecturer in Vocational Guidance in the Department of Education and Community studies at the University of Reading. He has written extensively in the field of computer assisted guidance.

Greg Robb is the Careers and Industry Manager at the Sir William Nottidge Technology School, Whitstable, Kent.

Mike Shaw is a Careers Information Officer with Staffordshire Careers Service and an Associate Tutor for Canterbury Christ Church College.

Christine Thomas is an independent private consultant, head of a careers curriculum unit and has substantial experience of working on careers programmes in a wide range of special schools.

Tony Watts OBE is Director of the National Institute for Careers Education and Counselling (NICEC) and a leading national figure in careers related research and development. He is also a Visiting Fellow at the University of London Institute of Education.

FOREWORD

This book is being published at an important time for careers education and guidance. There can never have been a period when interest in the subject has been higher.

At the end of the last century the aim was 'education for all'. At the end of this one it has become 'training for all'. It is not so long ago that the majority of young people leaving school, and especially young women, received no formal training and for this to be considered quite acceptable and proper. This is no longer the case, and it is vital that we make the most of our most important resource, people. In order to do this it is crucial that career decisions are made in the most informed and optimum way.

The nature of work is changing so that in the future people will be required to adopt different patterns of work; including self employment, fixed term contracts and frequent retraining, as technology changes and work structures adapt in response to ever greater international competition. All this puts a bigger emphasis on the skills of career management and in particular career decision making, thus presenting careers education and careers guidance with a more significant and substantial task. Such imperatives can make the need for careers education and guidance appear instrumental in character. There is no doubt a clear need to get it right for economic and technological reasons, just as there is for education in general, but there is also the equally vital purpose of helping each individual towards the fullest form of self-expression.

Books on careers education are quite a rarity, reflecting the marginal position it currently holds within education. It is rare for schools to have more than one person who is substantially involved and for that person to have had much more than brief initial training. Self-help is the way most practitioners progress. Books such as this therefore perform a valuable function. They represent landmarks in development by bringing together in one place, for new and experienced practitioners, the range of issues currently preoccupying the field.

Peter Heaviside
Department for Education
and Employment, 1995

INTRODUCTION

This book has been written at a time of unprecedented government policy initiatives aimed at raising the quality of careers education and guidance (CEG) offered to students in statutory schooling and beyond. The aim of this book, therefore, is to explore some of the key issues for practice and professional development which arise from these policy initiatives. It does so through providing insights into four aspects of careers work which are central to government concerns: changing the way in which the provision of careers guidance is managed; developing CEG through the curriculum; improving the quality of professional training for both teachers and careers advisers; and looking to ensure high standards of quality.

The contributors to this book have a diverse range of professional interests and experiences which provide a balanced view of policy, theory and professional practice in the field of CEG. The balance between these dimensions and their integration is crucial. In our view, achieving a qualitative change in careers work requires everyone working in this field to collaborate to pursue these three legitimate concerns. We believe this book suitably illustrates the way in which individuals can be empowered and yet contribute to the common good – a theme which has been loudly promoted by Sir Christopher Ball in recent years. His campaign has focused on the primacy of individual responsibility as a key factor in developing economic success for the nation. It has been argued that the nation's skill base and economic performance depends on every individual embracing the notion of life-long learning and becoming fully committed to the management and development of their own 'career'.

Tony Watts describes the influential role that the CBI has had in this debate, especially in promoting CEG as a vital strand in empowering individuals to take active responsibility for their own learning. The same precept is also enunciated by Jacquie MacDonald, whose chapter sets out the key principles of action planning. Her concern is also to reflect on the important issues of who owns the process. Andrew Edwards' chapter on post-16 careers guidance takes this issue further in stressing the particular importance of providing careers support tailored to the needs of individual learners through a cycle involving planning, review and feedback.

The need for individuals to become more active participants in their experience of learning in general, must equally apply to their experience of careers education and guidance. Peter Heaviside argues that guidance providers must take account of how individuals can learn from CEG. Individuals have preferences for the way they are helped and guidance providers should give this due attention. This is especially illustrated in Chapter 7, which describes how a UK Careers Service initiated a curriculum development project to underpin the guidance learning processes. Christine Thomas sets out some very practical examples of how experiential approaches can be achieved in working with students with learning difficulties, while Marcus Offer describes the role which the personal computer can play in making guidance more interactive and responsive to students' needs. Making CEG more interesting and immediate to the experiences of today's teenagers is the theme of Ken Fox's chapter. Few of us would underestimate the influence which television can have on young people's perception of the world and of the adult roles with which they identify. This chapter provides some useful insights into how such media can provide a rich source of shared experiences from which to explore work-related themes in the classroom.

The debate about empowering individuals is also linked to the way in which professional development and training in CEG is related to the needs of the teacher and careers adviser as individual learners. Bill Law's analysis of the Staff Development (SD) for Careers Work Project provides the important contextualisation for such a discussion and argues that effective staff development must also be concerned with the consequent need for changes in programme and organisational development. The responsibilities of all stakeholders in this process are brought to the fore.

David Frost proposes a model for professional development which makes a direct link between the individual's professional learning and the development priorities of their institution or organisation. For the past few years, this model has been linked to an award-bearing scheme which is described by reference to case studies in Chapter 12 (Reynolds and Frost). This serves almost as a microcosm for illuminating one of the other key themes emerging in this book – the management of change. The case studies which describe the experiences of learners and tutors alike, demonstrate the veracity of Law's earlier findings that change in one area must affect change in another. David Cleaton and Lesley Arnold's experience, described in Chapter 15, typify this principle on a much wider scale through their innovative work in the Seychelles. Hartley and Shaw describe how professional development also impacts upon change, in this case through careers advisers and careers teachers training alongside each other. They describe how an accredited programme provided a context for strengthening mutual support and understanding as well as building the confidence and competence of the practitioners concerned.

Both Tony Watts and Peter Heaviside pose some potential dilemmas for the partnership between schools and the Careers Service, following the privatisation of the latter. Watts is concerned that new funding initiatives for careers guidance do not upset the traditional balance between schools and the Careers Service, which has hitherto been built upon complementary expertise. Heaviside looks much more closely at how the new Careers Service will discharge its commitments and counsels against abandoning past practice too quickly, while at the same time, using a broader view of guidance which looks at educational routes and 'maps', not just goals. He recognises the inability of guidance providers to compensate for weaknesses in the opportunity structure, but believes that they do have an important role in informing those who control access.

Establishing effective change in CEG also depends upon teaching gaining the commitment and support of senior managers. Anthony Barnes sets out in Chapter 3 a case that demonstrates the value of CEG for the pupil, for the school and for society at large. Changing perceptions necessarily means changing and redefining terminology – exactly what do we mean by 'career'? Barnes argues that a wider definition of career, which refers to a student's evolving experiences of work roles and activities, may help gain more support for CEG.

Several writers also deal with issues surrounding evaluation of practice and quality. Policy initiatives are funded to achieve a 'step-change' in standards. More broadly, Barnes has provided a 'stakeholders' view of quality which places the learning needs of students at the centre. Heaviside also believes that guidance providers must be more open to evaluation of their practice, and be prepared to change accordingly.

Frost, however, is concerned with demystifying evaluation and allowing practitioners to implement practical strategies for improvement and change. He maintains that the opportunities for improving professional practice through evaluation are especially productive within a 'collegial' ethos. This means that the people directly involved in developing practice are those who undertake the evaluation – they collaborate to evaluate their own practice, in order to improve that practice. This model has been an implicit feature of the portfolio approach to assessment described in the case studies by Harber, Hewitt and Bannister.

One final theme that has featured strongly throughout these pages has been the influence and value of both *personal* networking – teachers, careers advisers, school inspectors/advisers, academics and higher education tutors, and *institutional* networking, between government departments, schools, careers services, professional associations and institutions of higher education. Recent government policy and funding initiatives have presented all members of this wider network with a major opportunity and challenge. It is the need to weld together a series of disparate measures through a process of professional dialogue and action which meets the interests of all stakeholders, most importantly the students themselves. Clearly it must do so in such a way which demonstrates that the personal, social and economic benefits of CEG are a genuine outcome of a collaborative working partnership between those concerned with policy, theory and practice. We hope this book is a contribution to that end.

Acknowledgements

We would like to record our sincere thanks and appreciation to all the contributors to this book, who, despite the pressure of their professional responsibilities, have found the time to reflect on their experiences and provide such valuable accounts of their practice. In addition, we thank Jo Walter for her expert adminstrative support and help with the editorial process.

David Frost, Andrew Edwards
and Helen Reynolds, 1995

The Context of Change

This section provides the background to
current developments in careers
education and guidance.

CHAPTER 1

CAREERS EDUCATION AND GUIDANCE IN SCHOOLS: POLICY AND PRACTICE

AG Watts

Careers education and guidance has recently received greater policy attention in Britain than ever before. The range of government initiatives in the guidance field is so extensive that it is difficult to keep abreast of them all. Together they provide a major opportunity to achieve a step-change in the extent and quality of careers provision. Whether this opportunity will be taken depends largely on the extent to which it is possible to weld the disparate initiatives into a coherent framework for development.

This chapter will attempt to analyse some of the reasons for the greater policy interest in careers education and guidance. It will then examine some of the main recent policy initiatives relating to careers work in schools. Finally, it will identify a number of unresolved issues.

The Policy Focus

The increased policy prominence of careers education and guidance stems in significant measure from the Confederation of British Industry's seminal report *Towards a Skills Revolution* (CBI, 1989). This report argued the case for a massive improvement in Britain's skill levels in order to compete in world markets. It also suggested that one of the main deficiencies of Britain's education and training system was that it had given the needs of providers higher priority than the needs of individuals. It accordingly argued that the way forward was to 'put individuals first' and to encourage them to develop their skills and knowledge throughout their working lives. It promoted 'careership' as a concept that should be applicable to *all* individuals, and it recommended that public funding for post-compulsory education and training should as far as possible be channelled through individuals rather than going direct to providers. In particular, it proposed a system of credits that would give all young people post-16 a publicly funded right to education and training, and control over the form it should take. It then viewed effective careers guidance as the essential means of ensuring that such individual decisions were well-informed, and proposed that it required a 'new rationale, reinvigoration and extra investment' (p.23).

The CBI followed this report with a series of further reports that amplified its analysis and prescriptions. These included *Routes for Success* (CBI, 1993a), which identified improved careers education and guidance as one of the four main 'building-blocks' for implementing the concept of 'careership'. They also included *A Credit to Your Career* (CBI, 1993b), which was devoted wholly to the steps needed to improve guidance provision. These steps included some applications of quasi-market principles to guidance delivery, in particular through the concept of guidance vouchers designed to stimulate choice and competition between guidance services.

The CBI's reports have had a considerable influence on government policy. Some parts of their analysis have received wide assent; other parts have proved more contentious. The first key element of the analysis, the need for a skills revolution, is widely accepted (eg, TUC, 1991). It has indeed been formally enshrined in the National Targets for Education and Training, which have been endorsed by a broad range of bodies. The second key element – the concept of funding education and training through individuals rather than direct to providers – is more controversial. The government has nonetheless launched a system of training credits for 16/17-year-olds leaving full-time education. It has also announced its intention to explore the possibility of extending this into a wider system of learning credits designed to cover the whole 16–19 age group (DTI, 1994).

These developments have provided the context for the third key element (from the perspective of this chapter): the increased policy significance of careers education and guidance. This has been widely welcomed, as have many of the CBI's detailed proposals in this area. Its proposals for applying quasi-market principles to guidance delivery have, however, been strongly contested. In the event, the government has gone some way down the quasi-market route, although less far than advocated by the CBI. The Trade Union Reform and Employment Rights Act 1993 retained a Careers Service with a statutory requirement to provide a free service to specified client-groups. But it removed the service from the control of local education authorities (LEAs), and gave the Secretary of State for Employment powers to determine what form arrangements for its operation should take. The model adopted in England and Wales has been competitive tendering for what are in effect monopoly contracts to provide statutory services in specified geographical areas. The government has also launched a series of initiatives for developing guidance services for adults who are outside the Careers Service's statutory client-groups, and these have included experiments in the use of guidance vouchers. The appropriateness and effectiveness of these quasi-market innovations is still in question (Watts, 1995).

Policy Regarding Careers Education and Guidance in Schools

For some time, the increased policy interest in careers education and guidance seemed to be bypassing schools. There were fears that the removal of the Careers Service from LEA control would weaken its partnership with schools. This danger was seen as particularly acute because the Technical and Vocational Education Initiative, the contractual nature of which had helped to keep careers work actively on schools' agenda, was coming towards its end.

Within the Department for Education, careers education and guidance had been marginalised. It had been omitted from the statutory National Curriculum, and defined as one of five cross-curricular themes that schools were encouraged to implement (NCC, 1990). The cross-curricular themes were however conceptually and structurally weak. The themes were neither coherent nor exhaustive: they were selected to represent particular lobbies and interests. Moreover, ministers were from the outset very sceptical about them, tending to view them as distractions from the main curriculum (Graham and Tytler, 1992). Plans to provide more detailed support materials, including help with welding the themes into a whole-curriculum model, were dropped. Explicit policy references to the cross-curricular themes ceased. Schools were encouraged to preoccupy themselves with the statutory curriculum and with narrowly defined academic performance as measured through attainment targets and performance in public examinations.

In this situation, the only significant initiatives to support careers education and guidance in schools came from the Employment Department. The careers information initiative, administered through Training and Enterprise Councils (TECs), provided additional resources to equip secondary schools and colleges with up-to-date careers libraries and computerised information (DES and DE, 1991). In addition, the pilot schemes for training credits (later retitled 'youth credits') recognised the need for enhanced funding for careers education and guidance. Indeed, an evaluation of the first phase of the pilots reported 'near universal agreement that the most tangible benefits of TCs [training credits] for young people, so far, has been the increase and improvement in careers information, guidance and planning in year 11 of school and beyond' (ED, 1993a, para.41).

Anxieties about the weakening of the partnership with schools that might stem from the reorganisation of the Careers Service was significantly alleviated by the publication of the *Requirements and Guidance for Providers* (ED, 1993b). This document gave considerable attention to the importance of links with schools and the forms they should take. This reassurance was strengthened in 1994 when it was announced that the Employment Department was to provide significant additional funding to Careers Services to support careers guidance in schools in years 9 and 10. This was followed a few months later by the announcement that still further funds were to be provided to improve the quality and coverage of careers guidance for pupils from age 13, and in particular to ensure that they had access to guidance from careers officers at ages 13/14, 15/16 and (for those remaining in full-time education) 17/18 (DTI, 1994).

These measures to enhance the role of the Careers Service in schools were linked in policy terms to the development of new vocational options, and the increasing concern regarding the tendency of some schools to bias guidance at 16 in order to encourage pupils to stay on – with the capitation advantages this brought to the school – rather than to move on to alternative learning opportunities elsewhere (HMI, 1992). The government was in a dilemma here. Its market philosophy meant that it was keen to encourage competition between schools and colleges. But it was also concerned to encourage young people to enter the new vocational options it was developing – notably modern apprenticeships. It saw increased access to impartial guidance through the Careers Service as being one of the means of resolving this dilemma.

The channelling of significant new funds to Careers Services ran the risk, however, of unbalancing the partnership between schools and the Careers Service which had been the basis of government policy on careers work in schools since the publication of *Working Together for a Better Future* (DES, DE and Welsh Office, 1987). This partnership was based partly on complementary *expertise*: careers officers with their expertise in individual interviewing; teachers with their expertise in delivering careers education within the classroom. It was also based partly on complementary *position*: teachers with their day-to-day contact with pupils; careers officers with their impartiality – both 'a fresh pair of eyes' in relation to pupils, and with 'no axe to grind' in relation to opportunities inside or outside the school (Watts, 1986). The enhanced funding for Careers Services, however, along with the erosion of careers education in schools due to the pressures of the National Curriculum and the neglect of the cross-curricular themes, posed serious dangers of encouraging schools to regard careers education and guidance as a service that could be left to an external agency rather than as a partnership in which they were active and equal partners.

Accordingly, steps began to be taken in 1994 to provide some complementary support for the schools side of the partnership. Careers education and guidance was the only one of the cross-curricular themes to be mentioned in the Dearing Review of the National Curriculum: its significance was particularly linked to the development of new vocational pathways post-14 (Dearing, 1994). The subsequent *Competitiveness* White Paper included, in addition to its enhanced funding for Careers Services, support for organising work-experience programmes in schools – a careers-related element of the school curriculum that was particularly threatened by the end of TVEI. It also propounded the concept of an 'entitlement to careers education and guidance', including provision by schools of a planned programme of education on post-16 education and training options, and on different types of jobs, which schools would be expected to set out in their prospectuses. It further stated that the OFSTED inspection programme would monitor schools' performance in this area against defined criteria (DTI, 1994). This was linked to some strengthening of references to careers education and guidance in OFSTED inspection guidelines (see Westergaard and Barnes, 1994).

Further developments included the announcement that careers education and guidance would be included as a GEST category for in-service training of teachers, with a broad definition to encourage development as well as formal training. This was supported by a NICEC enquiry, part-funded by the Department for Education and the Employment Department, into staff-development provision for careers work: this mapped existing provision and proposed a set of possible national targets in this area (Andrews, Barnes and Law, 1995). A new version of *Working Together for a Better Future* was published, under the title *Better Choices*, which set out ten principles for good quality careers education and guidance: these included 'a planned programme of careers education and guidance with measurable targets which ensure individual progression', and also 'a comprehensive service level agreement with the Careers Service' (ED/DfE, 1994).

Then, towards the end of 1994 it was announced that the School Curriculum and Assessment Authority would produce new guidelines on careers education and guidance to replace those produced earlier by the National Curriculum Council (1990). This was a remarkable decision. Many had feared that the government would take a minimalist view of SCAA's role, confining it to the statutory curriculum and leaving other elements of the curriculum for schools to decide on their own. The announcement represented the first clear infringement of this position, recognising that schools might require some support and encouragement in addressing these other areas of the curriculum. The fact that careers work was the first to break the line was clear further evidence of the government's increased policy interest in this area.

Finally, in a second *Competitiveness* White Paper, *Forging Ahead*, it was announced that the government would introduce legislation, with three main aims: to secure the provision of careers education in maintained schools; to make schools and colleges responsible for working with the Careers Service and providing facilities for them; and to ensure that young people received information on the full range of education and training options (DTI, 1995). The subsequent consultation paper (ED/DfE, 1995) indicated that the government was not seeking to specify the extent or content of the careers education programme, nor the form that the partnership with the Careers Service should take. The role of the legislation was thus to assure minimal provision, and to pass clear messages about the government's broad expectations.

Unresolved Issues

By mid-1995, then, it seemed that the main building-blocks were in place for significant improvement in the quality of careers work in schools. At the same time, however, the resource pressures on school budgets threatened to restrict schools' capacity to take advantage of this opportunity. The risk of unbalancing the partnership between Careers Services and schools remained. It was given added weight by the fear that the new contracts for the management of the Careers Service would not permit sufficient flexibility to enable open negotiation with schools, and also by the announcement that some of the contracts were to be awarded to private sector providers. These factors, along with the continuing market pressures on schools to retain pupils post-16, seemed likely to maintain tensions in the relationship between Careers Services and schools which might undermine the partnership rather than reinforce it.

A further unresolved issue was the place of careers education within the curriculum. The CBI (1993b) had argued that there should be a statutory slot for careers education within the National Curriculum. The government's announcement post-Dearing that it planned to make no further major changes in the structure of the National Curriculum until the next century removed this from the agenda. It left open the extent to which careers education should be delivered on a separate basis, as part of a personal and social education programme, or infused across the curriculum. The National Curriculum Council (1990) had legitimised all of these approaches, but had clearly emphasised an infusion approach, as it had in the case of the other cross-curricular themes. Whitty *et al* (1994), however, demonstrated the difficulties of infusing such themes into traditional subjects based on very different 'recognition rules', ie, rules about what teachers and pupils regarded as legitimate discourse within particular lessons. Yet splitting them off from traditional subjects was equally problematic. Moreover, the abandonment of the concept of cross-curricular themes, and the failure to replace it with any alternative whole-curricular model that could embrace not only careers education and guidance but also other areas of the curriculum that shared the same dilemmas (health education, moral education, education for citizenship, and the like), meant that the basic issues underlying the place of careers education within the curriculum were not being addressed at a policy level.

In the end, policy only provides a framework for what happens in schools. It channels resources and provides a frame for accountability; it also passes messages about what government regards as important. In the careers field, the weak nature of the currently available policy instruments leaves considerable latitude for schools to decide how much attention to pay to careers education and guidance and what form their approach to it should take. It is still possible for schools to marginalise careers work if they so wish. Despite all the policy initiatives, therefore, the issue of whether there is to be a significant improvement in careers education and guidance within schools continues to rest, in large measure, in the hands of teachers in general and headteachers in particular.

CHAPTER 2

CAREERS GUIDANCE AND CAREERS SERVICES: FACING UP TO CHANGE

Peter Heaviside

We each have a preferred way of dealing with the world. As a result, when confronted with a problem we tend to define it in a way which suits our preferred way of solving it. Educationalists will define problems in ways which lend themselves to educational solutions, engineers will seek engineering solutions and so on. Careers advisers are not immune. It is an inevitable consequence of people having different attributes, suited to different occupational environments, that we approach problems in different ways. The resulting occupational framework is the way we organise our interaction with the physical world to make best use of our human resource. It is also the main way we have of distributing wealth, so it needs to work well. Careers guidance helps to make it work. Occupational structures are not fixed; as they change, people have shown a remarkable capacity to adapt. All forecasts suggest such changes are likely to be greater in the future, which is bound to have consequences for careers guidance. This chapter is about these changes.

The view that, until recently, the past offered a largely stable occupational structure is commonly held, but perhaps not entirely correct. Seen from its impact on the life of individuals in western Europe, I am not certain that the social, political, economic, scientific and technological change of the first half of the century was not greater than that of the second half. History is a tricky business. Nevertheless, our ideas about guidance are changing and will need to change to reflect the changing nature of work and career. To judge how guidance should change, we should not rush to demean the practice of the past nor extrapolate too far the trends that we feel are emerging. One of the engines for progress is enthusiasm for new ideas, but the past is littered with long-forgotten mistakes and misjudgements, 'new' ideas that lead nowhere. Instead of trying to predict the future and shape the present to fit it, we should perhaps try to identify those characteristics that we know shape careers guidance today and that are likely to do so in future.

Seven Propositions in Search of a Theory

1. Careers Guidance is Shaped by the Structure of the Education System

The structure of the education system is a major determinant of guidance practice. When the majority of young people left school at 15 or 16 to seek employment, guidance practice was very different from now. Its focus, for many, was on immediate job opportunities rather than on long-term career progression.

Careers guidance in schools currently is shaped by the requirement for pupils to make decisions on what to study in years 10 and 11 at the end of year 9 and the need to make even more substantial decisions at the end of statutory schooling in year 11. Unlike most adults who seek guidance, the requirement to make a decision is forced on them even though in their year group there may be a difference of up to 12 months in their ages. This is at a time when their personal attributes are still emerging and developing rapidly. The requirement to make decisions to an imposed timetable makes the provision of personally focused guidance a considerable challenge.

It is unlikely that we will see a substantial change to the educational system pre-16 that will affect this timetable, although we can expect greater diversity in the range of courses available. The implication remains that the guidance process will need to be managed for a 'mass audience', while trying to reflect individual ages and stages of development. In the circumstances, this can only be achieved through guidance that extends over a considerable period of time. The challenge is to ensure that, as far as possible, this is experienced as progressive and cumulative.

To accommodate the wide range of development needs among young people, it would help if they were able to identify and practise the skills that arise from their careers guidance learning throughout the programme. To achieve this and, in particular, to bring a stronger element of personalised learning, much greater use of personal recording would be helpful. I think this is a key development area for guidance practice and one that fits well with guidance needs based on the way occupations and careers are changing. It also helps to focus attention on the learning that results from careers education and careers guidance, rather than the process. And it provides a stronger basis for evaluation.

2. Careers Guidance is Shaped by the Nature of Opportunities

Structures are important but so is the nature of the options. There are many ways to the same goal; selecting routes is therefore as much a part of careers guidance as selecting goals. Which route is appropriate will depend largely on personal circumstances and preferred learning styles. The routes may have cost implications for the individual, but they are also differentiated by the process of learning they use. In a well-organised system of opportunities, early experiences of learning should point to the appropriate route. Currently, the choice of route depends too much on tradition and prejudice rather than on its intrinsic character and the demands it makes of the learner. Careers guidance should challenge these perceptions and seek to influence decisions by helping clients to consider the nature of the learning provided.

Because of the diversity of routes, careers guidance increasingly needs to encompass educational guidance and include guidance about learning routes as much as goals, the distinction made between educational guidance and careers guidance is therefore not helpful.

3. It is Guidance 'to' as well as Guidance 'through'

This is one of the major debates of guidance, a source of conflict and confusion. Guidance 'to' is based on the notion that a career goal can be established based largely on the attributes of the individual, the demands of opportunities and a plan mapped out to achieve it. Guidance 'through' is based on the idea that guidance helps someone through a maze, where the 'goal' emerges only when the maze is successfully negotiated. The process, in this case, is not one of trying to determine an end goal, but more a case of seeking opportunities for further development based on current attainment and inclinations. It recognises that progress through a career involves lots of decisions at different ages and stages.

These respectively so-called 'differentialist' and 'developmentalist' approaches are often presented as being at odds, and practitioners tend to line up behind one approach or the other (depending on their preferred way of dealing with the world, I suppose). But is there a conflict? The difference may be no more than the nature of the goals being set. The differentialist goal is seen as an 'end position' at some distance from the present, the developmentalist goal is seen as the 'next step'. They both involve matching individual characteristics to the options available and they both involve making plans to implement decisions. Whether the goals set are long-term 'to' goals or short-term 'through' goals should be more a matter of circumstance and the client's 'preferred way of dealing with the world', than of the adviser's preference for a particular theoretical model. Not only do people have preferred ways of dealing with the world, they have preferred ways of being helped. Guidance practice should reflect this.

This will require providers of guidance to be more open about the way they work, so they can give clients a choice. There should be no mystery as to how guidance works.

4. Guidance is Shaped by the Resources Available

Since most guidance activities are labour intensive, guidance is expensive. We must be able to demonstrate 'value for money'. We should ask what is the effect we seek from guidance, can it be achieved more cheaply? For example, careers advisers like to do guidance interviews and, to be fair, clients seem to like them too, but do they offer best value? Can the effect be achieved more economically? Much guidance practice in Careers Services is based on focusing a limited resource around the single most important decision point for most pupils, which is year 11. Recent government initiatives, backed by additional funding, have attempted to focus more guidance on the earlier stages of career decision making; the choice of options at the end of year 9. The guidance process is thus becoming more extensive. It is crucial that guidance is able to demonstrate its effect. The evaluation of guidance practice is generally weak. When all Careers Services are provided under contract, it will acquire a new and even greater significance than now. The starting point for evaluating guidance practice should be a clear statement of purpose, linked to the resource employed to achieve it.

Evaluation has an aura of being technical, difficult and complex. It is not: evaluation is easy, provided the subject of the evaluation is clear, well defined and not over ambitious. As a result of evaluation, well-established guidance practice may be challenged, requiring a readiness to change among careers advisers, the same kind of readiness to change that they are currently trying to achieve with their clients. Systematic evaluation will enable careers guidance to keep abreast of the changes, which should shape its practice.

5. Guidance cannot Compensate for Failures in the Structure of Opportunities

Guidance is a lubricant, it helps the machine to work smoothly. If the machine has a design fault, the lubricant might prolong its life, but it cannot fix the flaw. One of the aims of the education and training system should be to provide students with learning experience, to gain insight into their abilities, interests and preferred learning styles. Progress in the system should be as clear and straightforward as possible. The aim should be to reduce formal guidance to a minimum. Careers guidance interviews cannot alter perceptions, generated by young people and their parents, over years of observing the workings of the education and training systems. That is why, for example, careers guidance on its own appears to have little impact on gender-based choices or the status given to 'A' levels, in the minds of young people and others.

Careers guidance is not a substitute for a coherent set of progression routes, we must be realistic about what it can achieve. But Careers Services are well placed to inform the structure of opportunities. They deal with all young people and all opportunity providers; they are well placed to spot trends and influence provision. Improving the structure of opportunities can solve more clients' career problems than individual guidance will ever achieve. Just as public health improved more when water supplies were cleaned up than when penicillin was invented.

6. Careers Guidance is not the same as Careers Education

The terms careers education and careers guidance have been run together so often, they have become almost one word, certainly one concept. While they clearly overlap, there are distinctions that can be made and which I think are useful to maintain.

Careers education is 'education about careers', education about the world of work and how people move within it. As a result, skills and knowledge are acquired which enable choices to be made and careers to be managed but the central outcome is learning. The outcome of careers guidance is that a choice is made, learning is incidental. The difference between the two is most clear when we consider their purposes; the processes they use overlap more. One way of thinking of careers guidance, is as the 'personalising' of careers education. Sometimes careers guidance with young people turns into careers education. This happens often during careers interviews, where the young clients are in effect not ready for guidance. This explains why sometimes the action agreed with careers officers is to take forward learning *about* careers, rather than learning how to *progress* their career idea.

What we mean by careers education and careers guidance has therefore got into something of a muddle. I suggest that it is helpful to differentiate between these complementary, mutually supportive but different activities, acknowledging that while processes are sometimes similar, purposes are different. This will provide a clearer focus for their development and sharing of responsibilities between Careers Services and schools. The trend towards merging careers education and careers guidance and talk of the learning outcomes of guidance has blurred a distinction that makes sense for the career preparation of young people. As a result of the muddle, guidance appears to have acquired the purposes of careers education which, in practice, careers advisers are not able to fulfil. Guidance has been distracted from its more narrow function of helping to effect a match between the requirements and resource of individuals and the demands of available opportunities.

7. Careers Guidance Requires Effort from Clients

Guidance is not a passive process for the client. For guidance to be effective, the client needs to work hard. Guidance is not the same as a medical examination and diagnosis where the client is largely passive. Guidance requires a fully participating client, who is prepared to study and research options; it involves working with complex decision-making processes and perhaps challenging strongly held views. None of this is easy. It has been estimated that applying for a university place requires at least 20 hours of work. There is an important task to be done to get this message across, since, if the new world of work requires individuals to take more responsibility for their careers and negotiate more changes than previously, then they will have to put more effort into their career management. We need to get this over to clients, who need to make time for it to manage it properly.

Summary

Careers guidance is relatively straightforward. The challenge of doing it well stems from the context within which it takes place, the need to balance conflicting demands and adjust for changing circumstances. This chapter has attempted to identify and characterise some of the contextual matters. In summary, they are:

- a system of education that requires decisions from all young people by particular dates;
- a range of opportunities that are differentiated more by prejudice and tradition than the differences in learning they offer;
- where careers guidance should be about 'through' as well as 'to', but where practitioners are not always clear about which their client needs;
- where resources are limited and the need to demonstrate value for money is high;
- where its role is as a lubricant, rather than a designer of the system;
- the need to distinguish between careers education and careers guidance, but for schools/colleges and Careers Services to work closely together; and
- the need for the clients to put effort into their guidance.

Implications

Careers guidance used to be seen as choosing a 'career *route*'. In future it should perhaps be seen as choosing a 'career *map*'. Choosing a piece of territory that meets the client's characteristics and requirements. This could be said to be careers guidance. And, alongside that, equipping clients with the 'map reading skills' they will need to range over the ground. This could be said to be careers education.

Guidance will, at least for the time being, need to use occupational titles. These are its currency, a shorthand for encapsulating individual requirements, but the aim should be to help clients see how their particular mix of attributes might be developed and used across an occupational territory. It will be crucial to help them understand how their attributes link with occupations, in ways that go beyond the distraction and often inhibiting factor of occupational titles.

So how are we to do this? For young people in school and college, careers guidance needs to build on an extensive and extended process of education. Careers guidance is less effective where it is not supported by good careers education. This finding goes back at least as far as a 1982 study that demonstrated that young people progressed further during the course of their guidance inter-views in those schools where there was a high level of Careers Service involve-ment in the careers education programme. A more recent study undertaken by the National Foundation for Education Research (NFER) on behalf of the Employment Department reinforces the finding (Morris and Stoney, 1995). The clear implication is that the Careers Service must in the first instance seek to support and help schools develop their careers education. Expert individual guidance cannot compensate for inadequate education preparation. We should be seeking to develop a more open educational process for guidance to complement careers education learning, rather than a confidential counselling one.

Training and Development

If this is the direction we are to go, and some Careers Services are already working/thinking is this way, then there are clear implications for training both careers advisers and careers coordinators. First, it suggests that there needs to be much more joint training. While teachers and careers advisers make distinctive contributions, the skills and, in particular, the knowledge they require overlap considerably. The most effective way to establish a shared understanding and common agenda is through joint training. Second, Careers Services need to be equipped to support curriculum development and delivery in schools. Third, careers advisers need to be able to operate in a guidance process that is not focused around an individual's guidance interview, but which sees that as part, albeit often a crucial part, of an extended learning process. Fourth, the need to be able to provide careers guidance that matches individual requirements and resources to appropriate educational and occupational goals, whether these goals are long-term 'to' goals or immediate 'through' goals. Finally, all careers advisers do not have to do everything that is expected of Careers Services. There is often a confusion between what is expected of individual careers advisers and the Careers Service as a whole. The Careers Service needs to be able to offer a range of services, each careers adviser does not need to provide all of these. There is scope for specialisation and there is scope for Careers Services to employ people with a range of expertise, to complete its portfolio of services to schools, colleges, employers and parents.

The current arrangements for training careers officers attempt to put too much into initial training, subsequent training is not sufficiently structured and careers teacher training is fragmented. The new NVQ structure provides a good opportunity to do something about this, by providing different levels of accredited training for all those who work in Careers Services and who are involved in careers work in schools and colleges.

Careers advisers, more than any other group, should be aware of how occupations are changing, including their own, and will need to change even further in future. Their clients will need to be flexible and adaptable to meet the demands of current and anticipated occupational structures, and so will they. This chapter suggests some ways in which this might be achieved. On the other hand, they could just be my preferred way of dealing with the world.

Note: The views expressed in this chapter are personal to the author and do not necessarily reflect those of the Department for Education and Employment.

CHAPTER 3

WHAT GOVERNORS AND MANAGERS NEED TO KNOW

Anthony Barnes

Consultants working with schools and Careers Services in central London summarised the lot of careers coordinators in the following way. They are:

- mostly subject specialists – careers is only part of their work;
- have very limited time for their careers work;
- have very limited resources for their careers work;
- usually not trained in careers;
- often young and inexperienced, without much guidance on good practice;
- professionally isolated – having little contact with other careers teachers;
- institutionally isolated – with no obvious allies or chains of support within schools;
- unsupported (except in lip-service) by senior management and governors;
- often enthusiastic, and most would like to do a better job, if enabled to do so.

Many careers teachers will be able to recognise some or all of these elements in their own situation. There are, of course, schools and areas where the picture is less depressing. Within London, and other parts of the country, there are well-qualified careers coordinators, reasonably well resourced to do the work, functioning at a strategic level within the school and operating effectively within external networks, to support the career development of students. Nevertheless, it remains a cause of concern that quality and standards remain as patchy as they are. This chapter provides a guide for governors and senior managers, who would like to bring the practice in careers education and guidance in their school up to the level of the best.

Why Bother?

Inevitably, the first step is to persuade those governors and managers, who still need convincing, that careers education and guidance requires strengthening. The arguments may be marshalled around four principal assertions.

1. It's Good for Students

The purpose of careers education and guidance is to equip students with the skills, attitudes, knowledge and experience that will help them to manage their lifelong career development. By developing themselves and their capabilities, particularly through investing in their own learning, they will have a better chance of making progress and experiencing success in their working lives, however these may be defined. By investigating the challenges and opportunities of working life, they may develop wider career horizons and higher aspirations. By acquiring the skills of enquiring, planning and deciding, they will be better prepared to weigh up advice and information, take responsibility for their career plans and make successful transitions from school to further and higher education, training and work.

2. It's Good for Society

Careers education and guidance has social, economic and political value. Careers education, for example, can help students to understand and assess where they stand on a range of complex issues associated with careers and work. Society is faced with many difficult questions relating to issues such as fostering enterprise, promoting equality of opportunity, the exploitation of labour, safeguarding the environment, valuing different kinds of work and sharing access to it. Students, as the young citizens of today, need opportunities to discuss changing career and work patterns and structures. Careers guidance can help students to choose wisely, avoid costly mistakes and aspire to higher levels of education and training.

3. It's Good for the School

Careers work helps students to understand the 'skills sets', such as personal, interpersonal, communication and numeracy skills, which are developed through the curriculum. Understanding the relevance to their own career prospects of progressive development of the core skills that are helpful in most, if not all, kinds of work, can help to improve students' motivation, staying power, attendance and achievement.

Studies also show a link between 'career decidedness' and higher levels of motivation and achievement. 'Decidedness' does not mean premature vocational specialisation or unwise narrowing down of options. Indeed, planned procrastination – deciding not to decide – where a student makes a conscious decision to delay making a choice, has also been found to help students achieve. The worst scenario is when students feel anxious or dispirited about their career prospects.

High-quality provision of careers education and guidance can improve students' and parents' confidence in the school. There is little evidence that parents of prospective students rate careers work highly in their list of priorities when selecting a school. However, they do express an interest if they are shown round an attractive and well-functioning careers library on the headteacher's initial tour of the school, or on Open Day. Parental surveys can sometimes reveal unexpected sources of disquiet with the quality of the careers provision. These can often be easily remedied and parental satisfaction restored.

4. You Have to Do it Anyway

This is the argument of last resort, the equivalent of the harassed parent disciplining a recalcitrant child. The strict legal requirement is limited. Secondary schools are required to publish in the prospectus details of the careers education and guidance provided and the arrangements for work experience (DfE Circular 14/94). The 1993 Education Act required schools to provide year 11 pupils with information that is published by the further education sector. In addition, the Parent's Charter states that schools should make available information on all options for 16-year-olds, and that careers teachers and the Careers Service should be ready to answer parents' questions at any time during their children's schooling. Schools have a duty to uphold the law on sex discrimination (1975) and race relations (1976); and the Code of Practice, issued by the Commission for Racial Equality, reminds schools that it is unlawful to discriminate against pupils in matters relating to careers advice and work experience.

In recent years, many schools have responded positively to the external pressure to strengthen careers provision, which has come from a number of directions including the Technical and Vocational Education Initiative (TVEI) and the changes linked to the restructuring of Careers Services. In 1994–5, an even more dramatic shift in the direction of national policy has been discernible. It was prefigured in the final report by Sir Ron Dearing on the review of the National Curriculum (Dearing, 1995), which made several prominent references to the importance of careers education at key stages 3 and 4. It was reinforced by the *Better Choices* booklets (DfE/ED, 1994, 1995), which exhorted key partners in the provision of careers education and guidance to work together to meet young people's needs and *Looking Forward* (SCAA, 1995), which offered advice with curriculum planning. The intention to strengthen careers education and guidance in schools was announced in the White Paper on *Competitiveness: Forging Ahead* (DTI, 1995). The proposals included legislation, following consultation, to improve careers education and guidance in schools; and the strengthening of the OFSTED Framework of Inspection, to ensure that inspectors seek evidence that schools have provided good careers education and impartial guidance.

These arguments may remain unconvincing for any number of reasons. One possible reason for resisting the arguments offered here, is a different understanding of the nature of 'career'. The term is used in everyday speech with different meanings, although this rarely gives rise to misunderstanding because it is understood in its context. Careers education and guidance may be perceived as less important if career is understood to refer to progression within an organisational hierarchy. This is a very narrow definition related to a pattern that is now much less widespread. The rationale for careers education and guidance in the curriculum is based on a wider definition of career, which refers to the evolving experiences of work roles and activities of every student. This is a far cry from the notion that some students may not have careers at all. Every student will have a career that they, and not an external organisation, are responsible for managing. Defined in this way, it becomes much more important for schools to assist students to optimise their career prospects, by encouraging them to invest in their own learning for lifelong career development. This argument applies whether or not students leave school at 16 or continue in education and training. Although students may not enter employment until their early twenties, they will still benefit from a planned programme of careers education and guidance that helps them to understand the changing patterns of careers, the changing nature of work and prepares them to manage their own career development throughout their lives.

Policy

Senior managers and governors have a key role in determining the place of careers education and guidance in the school's aims. To achieve this, they need to take into account the viewpoints of the principal stakeholders – those who have a legitimate interest in the goals that the school pursues, and how it accomplishes them. Students, parents, staff, employers, training and enterprise councils, local education authorities and central government, are among the stakeholders who may have widely differing priorities regarding the purposes of the school. Differences of outlook within the same interest group may add to the sense of ambiguity. Nevertheless, senior managers and governors have to strive for a consensus and agreement on the scope and value of careers in school aims and try to ensure that this is carried through into the school ethos and values system. Section 1 of the Education Reform Act (1988) is a good starting point, with its definition of the duty of schools to prepare pupils for the opportunities, responsibilities and experiences of adult life.

A school policy on careers education and guidance should spring from the school's aims. While the careers coordinator may advise on the possible content of such a policy, senior management and governors need to make fundamental decisions about the design of the school curriculum and how and when careers education and guidance will be offered to students. They also need to approve the policy, and ensure that the process of policy-formulation contributes to building consensus and support from all those who will be responsible for its implementation. A policy needs to be reviewed regularly and to include:

- a statement of the aims and purpose of careers education and guidance in the school, based on students' entitlement;
- a commitment to supporting other whole school policies, particularly those for personal and social education, equal opportunities, multi-cultural education and special needs;
- a brief description of how the policy will be managed and evaluated, and the physical and human resources that will be allocated for its implementation, including a commitment to addressing the staff development needs of those involved;
- a commitment to working in close partnership with the Careers Service to ensure students' access to impartial guidance; and to working with parents, businesses and the wider community in order to secure learning opportunities for students.

A Development Plan

While a policy contributes to the vision and sense of direction, its practical value is to provide a reference point for the framing of priorities for development in careers education and guidance. Senior managers and governors can help to ensure that provision does not stand still or atrophy by proposing that careers has a development plan to promote change and improvement, like any other area of the curriculum. It is important to avoid the extremes of development and to devise a plan that is achievable but challenging. A summary of the development plan will need to state for each target, what tasks are involved, who will carry them out and by when, what resources will be needed and what are the criteria that will be used to evaluate the school's success in achieving the target. Schools may find it helpful to link the development plan for careers to the negotiation of a service level agreement with the Careers Service.

Appointment of Staff

The quality of careers education and guidance in the school can be influenced greatly by the appointment of suitable specialist staff to manage, coordinate and provide careers teaching and guidance on a day-to-day basis. In England, relatively few careers vacancies are advertised nationally and filled by external applicants. Senior managers often prefer to select an existing member of staff, whom they know will have the personal qualities to carry out the work sympathetically and efficiently. Sometimes appointments to careers work are made for less laudable reasons with profoundly unsatisfactory consequences. Schools benefit from having a careers coordinator who is well respected by students, parents, the Careers Service and employers who work directly with the school. This places a responsibility on senior management and governors to try to identify a suitable member of staff and to ensure that they have sufficient status and time to be effective in the role. The careers coordinator also needs to possess sufficient expertise, or to have the potential to develop it. At the moment, relatively few teachers have a formal qualification in careers work. This is beginning to change as the availability of training spreads and government funding is directed to support training, including approaches based on the assessment of competence.

The process of appointing a careers coordinator begins with the writing of a job description, which defines the purpose of the job, and a person specification, which describes the qualities, skills, experience and commitment needed by the individual. Senior managers and governors may find it helpful to clarify what they require of a coordinator under a number of headings.

- *Managing upwards*. Coordinators may advise senior managers and governors on the policy for careers and its place in the overall curriculum offered. They may need to recommend priorities for development and to contribute to negotiations with the Careers Service.
- *Managing sideways and downwards*. Coordinators may need to work cooperatively and productively with colleagues on developing and implementing careers education and guidance in the curriculum. They may chair careers team meetings and curriculum working groups. From time to time, they may be involved in organising and providing teaching resources and training for staff.
- *Managing inwards*. Coordinators need to be well-organised, manage their time well and cope with the peaks and troughs in their workload.
- *Managing outwards*. Coordinators work closely with the Careers Service and develop and maintain links with employers and the wider community.
- *Providing careers teaching and learning activities*. Coordinators need to work with colleagues to devise opportunities for CEG across the curriculum.
- *Providing careers guidance activities*. Coordinators work closely with Careers Service to ensure that students have access to high-quality, impartial guidance.
- *Managing and organising the provision of careers information*. Coordinators take responsibility for the selection and presentation of up-to-date careers information, which is free of stereotype.

It is likely that the role of the coordinator will vary from school to school depending on its particular needs. It is also the case, for example, that the role of a newly appointed coordinator will change as the person becomes more experienced. This makes it even more important that the potential for development of the applicant is taken into account.

In considering the person specification, it is important to ensure that the applicant:

- can demonstrate genuineness, empathy and regard for students;
- is willing and able to promote equal opportunities;
- is committed to investing in their own training and development.

The role of senior management and governors goes beyond the appointment of the careers coordinator or teacher. Careers staff need the support of a line manager, not only for appraisal purposes, but also to be pro-active in developing this area of the curriculum. One of the most frequently recorded difficulties is the isolation felt by the careers coordinator. The line manager can help the coordinator tap into the decision-making structures and processes in the school. Another source of valuable support is to make it possible for careers staff from all the local schools to meet together on a regular basis, in order to take part in staff development activities that they have arranged for themselves.

Quality and Standards

Senior management and governors may adopt a range of approaches to securing and maintaining high quality and standards. The standards or criteria for recognising good quality provision may be developed internally, as for example in the development plan for careers, or adopted from outside. In several areas of the country, kite-marking schemes have been devised to recognise the achievement of schools in meeting locally agreed standards for careers education and guidance. Such schemes may be attractive to schools for the public recognition that they give and for the measure of external objectivity that they provide. Inspection may serve a similar function and has a part to play alongside other methods.

A Wider Role

Senior managers and governors may be able to contribute to the direct teaching activities within the careers programme. For other staff, the knowledge that the headteacher or a deputy wishes to teach on the programme, sends an important signal to them that careers is no less important than the examined curriculum.

Governors, through their contacts in the community, may be in a position to identify resources and contacts for the careers programme. In a growing number of schools, a member of the governing body takes on a special responsibility for working closely with the careers coordinator.

Towards the Millennium

The targeting of senior managers and governors as holding the key to improving careers education and guidance is clearly made in *Better Choices*. All of the ten principles for good quality careers education and guidance implicitly or explicitly depend on strategic decisions and actions. The principles for good quality careers education and guidance in schools and colleges from *Better Choices* are set out below.

1. A coordinated approach to the management of pupil and student development.
2. A written whole school or college careers education and guidance policy.
3. Management training for headteachers and principals to include careers education and guidance.
4. Clearly defined school/college senior management support, including a named person responsible for careers education and guidance.
5. A comprehensive service level agreement with the career service.
6. Appropriate resources for the delivery of an effective programme.
7. A planned programme of career education and guidance with measurable targets that ensure individual progression.
8. Regular review and evaluation.
9. Input from parents, governors, employers, training providers and others.
10. Planned in-service training for teachers, lecturers and careers advisers.

Over 20 years earlier, inspectors had produced a list of ten features of schools providing good careers education (HMI, 1973). It makes an interesting comparison. It was largely concerned with technical issues, most of which remain just as valid today, but the emphasis on strategic management was completely lacking. In the intervening years, the attention given to the role of senior management was very sporadic. Catherine Avent, senior inspector for careers education and guidance with the Inner London Education Authority, was one of the few who wrote advice for headteachers on carrying out their role in relation to careers work. *Better Choices* has had a considerable impact. In many parts of the country, senior managers accompanied their careers coordinators to the local meetings at which *Better Choices* was launched. It remains to be seen to what extent this momentum is maintained and leads to further strengthening of the management of careers education and guidance.

Developing the Curriculum

This section outlines a number of
developments that demonstrate ways in
which careers education and guidance
can become established in the
curriculum.

CHAPTER 4

CAREERS EDUCATION AND GUIDANCE AND THE ACTION PLANNING PROCESS

Jacquie MacDonald

This chapter will explore how action planning can play an integral part in the delivery of a careers education and guidance programme, and explain how the principles of careers education and guidance closely relate to the principles and processes of action planning. Action planning can provide a coherent framework for the practical application of any careers programme, which in turn should be enhanced by the student's record of achievement and action plan.

Action planning and individual action plans have become widely used terms to describe the process and product of target setting within education, training and, increasingly, in the workplace. Setting personal targets is now seen as an important and integral part of teaching and learning.

What is Action Planning?

A clear rationale for action planning has recently been articulated in the CBI document *Towards a Skills Revolution: A Youth Charter* (CBI, 1989). This addressed the issue of improving student motivation and participation in post-16 education and training. Action planning was perceived as a major strand of this initiative.

Action planning is the process by which students review the present, set goals for the future and identify strategies by which the goals can be achieved. It increases students' self-awareness by providing an opportunity for them to review their current situation, responsibilities, experiences and skills. It provides a means for managing transitions by supporting students in clarifying their needs, examining their options and identifying 'next best actions'. In essence, action planning is a process that aims to enable individuals to take control of their own learning, achieve a better understanding of their experiences and decide future actions. In broad terms, there are three strands to action planning; educational, personal/social and vocational.

- *Educational action planning* tends to cover general school issues like homework, completing set assignments, as well as approaches to learning and behavioural targets that may be linked to any particular subject.
- *Personal/social action planning* focuses on attendance, punctuality, attitude, behaviour, as well as hobbies, interests, and extra curricular activities.
- *Vocational action planning* is most closely related to careers guidance. It may involve identifying information seeking skills or activities, such as work experience, which aim to clarify vocational choices. It also has a transitional element, for example, moving from primary to secondary school and from year 9 to year 10 (a GCSE programme).

Action Planning, Learning and Skills Development

The process of action planning should be an integral part of learning support in all areas of the curriculum. For maximum effectiveness, there should be a whole institution approach to action planning. Good practice should also allow the individual to take some control of their learning targets and development. It should aim to raise expectations and motivate individuals towards 'next best actions', building on success, remedying failures.

Action planning itself facilitates the development of self-awareness, self-reflection, self-confidence and self-esteem. It develops decision-making skills by providing a supportive, systematic framework in which the individual can appraise themselves and evaluate future actions. Where action planning is developed lower down the school it allows time for students to practise and rehearse these skills before they have to make 'serious' decisions.

Action Planning and CEG

So far I have looked at action planning largely as an educative process and have focused on its capacity to increase student motivation and develop skills that have a lifelong application. I would now like to address its relationship to careers education and guidance. The process of action planning provides the individual with some key questions that link with the principles of careers education and guidance work, such as:

- Where am I now in terms of achievement? *(self-awareness)*
- What are my aims? *(decision making + opportunity awareness)*
- What do I need to do in order to achieve my aims? *(decision making)*
- What support do I need? *(interpersonal skills + decision making)*
- What timescale am I talking about? *(transition skills)*

- What action do I take? *(self-awareness + decision making)*
- How am I doing, is there a need to review my aims? *(self-awareness, decision making skills + transition skills)*

Both careers work and generic action planning can therefore help the individual to:

- develop skills in planning, target setting, negotiating and reviewing;
- focus on academic, vocational and/or personal goals;
- assess progress and areas requiring development;
- participate in a structured programme that includes access to appropriate information and support materials, and access to impartial advice and informed guidance.

Both careers work and action planning involve reflecting and reviewing experiences and looking towards future plans. Both aim to:

- help the individual to evaluate their interests, aptitudes and abilities (self-awareness);
- ensure that the individual is fully aware of the complete range of opportunities available (widening horizons/opportunity awareness);
- enable students to develop strategies and skills for making realistic decisions for themselves (making choices/decision-making);
- enable the individual to develop the skills of transition and identify and use support structures (transition skills).

For some young people, career decisions result from the combined help and support they receive through an informal and formal guidance network. This can result in resistance to more systematic action planning. The Audit Commission report, *Unfinished Business* (Audit Commission/OFSTED, 1993) indicated that, among several possible factors, the lack of guidance individuals receive at the transition stage may have contributed to the large drop-out rate on post-16 courses. This, together with the growth in vocational courses, suggests that action planning, target setting and careers education should be an integral part of all work-related programmes, such as the General National Vocational Qualification (GNVQ) and the Youth Award Scheme.

Action Planning and the Careers Programme

An effective careers programme that incorporates action planning generally starts by identifying the needs of a specific year group. This may be followed by a review of the aims and objectives of the programme in question which sets out a list of activities and learning objectives. This involves activities that take place under the heading of careers work and other events that take place as part of a school's programme. For example, a careers education module for year 10 students might entail:

- a review of year 9 and action planning and target setting for year 10;
- information-seeking skills, developing library and computer skills;
- school assemblies, special event days, careers conventions;
- guidance talks from Careers Service staff in small groups followed by individual interviews;
- exploring job knowledge, interest families and training opportunities;
- updating on self-awareness by a further exploration of strengths, areas of interest and areas requiring development;
- action planning in preparation for work experience, where the action plan sets out what the student might hope to gain from the work experience;
- job study project;
- visiting speakers including past students and speakers from non-traditional jobs;
- opportunities post-16, including changing labour market trends;
- preparation of a work experience statement for the National Record of Achievement (which reinforces the importance of action planning and progression through education);
- a review of year 10 achievements and an action plan for entry into year 11.

The aim is for each student to have the opportunity of work experience, discussion with a careers officer on career ideas and transition routes, participation in group sessions aimed at increasing self-awareness and self-confidence, and individual discussion with tutors about their general academic and personal development.

A Whole Institution Approach to Action Planning

In order for action planning to be effective it is important that the whole institution is involved. While individual tutors and subject teachers may undertake valuable action planning with a few students, more benefit can be gained from integrating action planning across the whole curriculum and involving the whole staff. This is particularly important as students may set targets that require the assistance and support of subject teachers as well as personal tutors or careers staff. All teachers have a role in action planning and careers work. The new emphasis is on the formalisation of the process as well as the learning outcomes, and the staff team need to consider from the outset the following issues.

1. *Implementing action planning.* Action planning and careers work need to be developed over a period of time and to build on existing teaching and learning programmes where review and target setting feature.
2. *Staff development.* There is a need for staff development to ensure that referral networks are established, understood and used and that staff themselves develop the relevant skills.

3. *Student overload.* Should students produce several action plans for different situations? What purposes do they serve? How often should students complete an action plan?
4. *Integration.* How is the action planning process and documentation to be integrated with other institutional programmes of assessment, personal, social and vocational education and related activities?
5. *Audience.* Is it a public or a private document? Perhaps there should be different versions.

It is easier to address these issues where there is a common agreement that schools should seek to establish a balanced and broadly based curriculum that 'prepares pupils for the opportunities, responsibilities and experiences of adult life', and that careers education and action planning should contribute to a whole school policy for the personal and social development of all its students. The staff team can then draw up a detailed plan of activities and processes to identify the:

- various stages of the educational and guidance process where action planning is appropriate;
- documentation required for reviews;
- resources available to help students engage with this activity;
- role played by other agencies involved in student guidance, notably the Careers Service;
- type of classroom activities that can be related to specific events, such as work experience, careers conventions and option choices;
- system for making referrals for individual guidance (educational, personal or career related);
- access to information on further education, training or work options;
- links with the National Record of Achievement process.

Case Studies: Action Planning in Action

School A

Action planning was introduced as part of a careers action plan for transition with a pilot group of year 11 students unfamiliar with action planning. The concept was introduced using an activity, 'Directions: going far', taken from London's Docklands pack 'Looking Forward'.

The activity aims to help students explore their hopes and ambitions for the future, to consider the influence of parents and others on their choices, and to give tutors an insight into students' thoughts and feelings so that additional help/counselling can be arranged if necessary.

Students are asked to brainstorm and describe one of their ambitions. Some groups found it easier to write these down. Students are given a set of 'Going far' cards describing statements about hopes and ambitions, a template and four blank cards. The students use the template to arrange the statements cards in order of personal importance. Students eventually have to reject four of these statements, and they can also use the four blank cards provided to write their own statements if they prefer. The statements on the cards relate to everyday life and include:

- supervise others at work;
- find someone I love;
- have lots of leisure time;
- be financially independent;
- find a good home;
- go to college;
- have a secure job;
- be my own boss;
- be famous;
- get good qualifications.

This exercise is done twice. Students first arrange the statements in order of the importance that they think their parent/guardian would prefer. Next, they arrange the statements in the order they choose. Both exercises provide an opportunity for them to discuss their own hopes and ambitions as well as those which they think their parents might hold for them. Students then record on a summary sheet:

- their personal hopes and ambitions (1st choice and 2nd choice);
- how they anticipate meeting these aspirations;
- how far they would like to go in terms of their hopes and ambitions;
- the hopes/ambitions of parent(s)/guardians/others.

The school found this a very useful starter exercise and hopes to extend this activity to the whole year group in preparation for transitional action planning sessions with careers advisers. In the long term, the aim is to adapt the activity as an educational action plan so that the task could be introduced in year 9 in preparation for student transition from Key Stage 3 (KS3) to KS4. As a follow up, two other proformas were designed and will form part of the second phase of development work at the school.

School B

(A School for Pupils Aged 11–19 with Severe Learning Difficulties)
The focus at KS4 and post-16 is on work-related activities and individual action plans. Courses at the school are devised to improve pupils' awareness about the adult world and to help prepare them for leaving school. The course involves visits, invitations to people to come for tea to talk about their work, role play activities and class based activities using careers resources to explore the theme of work and work skills. The work-related courses have been devised to involve pupils in planning and recording their own work. The course sheet has a

description written by the teacher, and a logo, picture or symbol to help the pupil understand which course it refers to. Individual aims for each pupil are discussed and agreed with the pupil when appropriate. At the end of the course the teacher adds a report to the sheet and this record is then kept in the student's course file and may be chosen by him/her for inclusion in the summative record of achievement. For many courses, the student will also be helped to complete a course review sheet, which asks 'How well did you work?' and looks at 'next steps', 'with my class', 'with my teacher', 'at home by myself'. The student may use a symbol-writing programme on the computer that can be accessed by pressing symbols or pictures on a concept keyboard.

Pupils in the KS4 group are learning to plan and evaluate opportunities using access materials. Individual aims and objectives are set and agreed by the staff, working with parents and students as appropriate. At the annual review, a list of generic aims is drawn up which forms the basis for the year's Individual Action Plan. This is translated into symbol form to help the student remember their goals.

Previously, the school introduced an individual action planning course module whereby individual pupils were shown how to choose an activity, plan it, carry it out and record it. This was done using symbols and computers in cooperation with parents. All pupils were asked to think of an activity that they would like to do, for example, at home. Ideas were kept simple and familiar – they then recorded what they wanted to do and took this record home to their family. The family were able to indicate whether they had been able to do their chosen activity and the student could then record that information back in school. This helped students to use text and symbols as a means of communication and it also taught them how to plan and develop a sense of control.

The school intends to make video tapes for each student with extracts from their school career to be included in their record of achievement on leaving school. Staff will include a short piece of video each year for every student.

School C

(Single Sex Girls LEA School taking part in the Technical and Vocational Education Initiative)

With the use of TEC funding, the school has piloted action planning as part of its PSHE (Personal, Social and Health Education) programme with students at Key Stage 4. Tutors introduced the concept of action planning to students in Year 11 who were asked to complete a booklet *Focus on the Future*. Symbols as well as written text were used to enable all students to participate.

Students completed a quick checklist based on how they were doing in each subject. This was followed by questions such as: 'Which subjects do you most enjoy?', 'Can you tell me about some pieces of work you have been proud of in those subjects?', 'Can you identify particular areas that you would like to improve?' Students were also given a 'Help sheet', which looks at long-term aims and short-term targets en route.

The evaluation at the end of the pilot indicated that:

- students felt that they were being listened to and taken seriously;
- students felt they needed to be more responsible for themselves;
- students found it useful when they were given help and advice on how to achieve targets;
- students felt proud and quite pleased to have made improvements and were keen to set new targets.

However, the school feels that there are still issues to be addressed including the greater involvement with parents and the need to start action planning in year 7.

Conclusion

In summary, a quality careers education programme and action planning process are likely to be successful when:

- the individual is placed at the centre of the decision-making process;
- it is well planned and implemented and is linked to other initiatives;
- all those involved in the process are trained in the necessary skills;
- it forms part of a whole institution approach;
- it has the involvement and backing of senior management within the organisation;
- the process and principles are monitored and evaluated;
- objective information and informed guidance are available at the appropriate time.

Ideally, action planning and careers education should be viewed as a lifelong process and, therefore, an ongoing part of every individual's educational experience.

CHAPTER 5

POST-16 CAREERS GUIDANCE: THE ROLE OF TUTORIAL METHODS IN SUPPORTING GOOD PRACTICE

Andrew Edwards

So far this decade, one of the most prominent trends in post-16 education has been the steady and unprecedented increase in students continuing in full-time education beyond statutory schooling. Whatever explanations are offered for this phenomenon (Spours, 1992; Raffe, 1992), it has occurred at a time of widespread policy debate on how best to establish a 'learning pays' (Ball, 1991; 1992) culture, as well as a curriculum structure capable of creating alternative, but progressive opportunities for all students; a policy objective currently expressed through the expansion of General National Vocational Qualifications (GNVQs) and the introduction of modern apprenticeships.

During the same period, the education and training system has increasingly had to engage with a changing economic context, characterised by new technologies and the growing integration of world markets, with all of its attendant implications for the British labour market (Finegold, 1992; Ashton, 1992). Witness, too, the rapid expansion in higher education, and we are sharply reminded of the pressures students face in making the 'best choice available' at the post-16 and post-18 stages of their careers. Certainly, the economic cost of 'unsatisfactory' decisions has not been lost on policy makers (Audit Commission/OFSTED, 1993). Neither, of course, can the social costs be minimised. Guidance, therefore, almost by default, is becoming a more complex process. To those entrusted with guiding students through a potential 'maze' of pathways, courses and labour market trends, it presents a challenge of equal magnitude. And we are yet to determine whether publicly funded careers guidance, delivered within the context of market-led reforms, will be equal to the task.

This scenario therefore suggests a somewhat urgent need to re-assess how the guidance needs of post-16 students can best be met. Simply providing more of the same cannot guarantee improvements in the quality of guidance provision. Rather, we need to re-examine the interdependence that exists between providing effective guidance on the one hand, and effective strategies for teaching and learning on the other. If learning pays, then guidance must pay also.

Yet while much of the literature associated with the post-16 debate enthusiastically endorses the need for improved guidance, there has been little in practice to suggest how this should be achieved. In 1994, the government White Paper, *Competitiveness, Helping Business to Win* (DTI, 1994), set out an entitlement to careers education and guidance for students aged 17 to 18. Although the additional funding promises to create increased activity by careers advisers, it was, nevertheless, quite modest in scope: 'Every young person remaining in full-time education will be offered further information and guidance by the Careers Service on post-18 choices.' (DTI, 1994, p.15)

The contribution that the Careers Service can make to meeting the widening guidance needs of students should be significant. A key question, however, is whether its conventional role is sufficient, either on its own or in conjunction with whatever careers programmes institutions provide by themselves. Improving practice, moreover, has to take account of certain other realities.

- Provision for the 11–16 group tends to be better coordinated, since most frequently, a member of staff has been given a specific responsibility for careers work, whereas in sixth forms, it is often unclear who has responsibility for careers. In colleges, the position is sometimes polarised between subject and student services departments.
- Common to both schools and colleges, is the fact that little curriculum time is available for careers work post-16.
- Careers work often focuses more upon the needs of students aspiring towards higher education than those intending to pursue other options (Whiteside, 1994, p.384).
- Careers inputs tend to be information orientated and linked to particular points in the course.
- There is limited scope to tailor the careers programme to the needs of individual students. Everyone gets the same thing irrespective of whether they need it or want it.
- Published resources for post-16 careers work are not particularly designed to support individual enquiry and tutorial work.

This description will ring true for some practitioners and less so for others. But it accurately portrays the situation for many, who recognise that both tutors and students need to be given more help and support as they engage in the guidance process (FEFC/OFSTED, 1994). I am arguing here that the small group tutorial can provide an especially useful context for enhancing guidance work with students. It also enables methods such as supported self-study to be an effective tool in stimulating enquiry and reflection.

The Tutorial Process

In practice, tutorials are used for a variety of purposes, normally associated with action planning, recording achievement and reviewing either personal, social or academic targets agreed between the tutor and his/her students. Additionally, tutorials sometimes play a key part in the use of flexible learning methods, such as supported self-study, whose methods and curriculum approach are intended to make effective use of the tutorial cycle.

The tutorial cycle also provides an opportunity to implement certain pedagogic principles which, unsurprisingly, also constitute an implicit part of effective guidance practice. These principles should enable students to:

- be more active and have more control in meeting their guidance needs;
- be more involved and consulted in assessing what help is appropriate;
- learn pertinent 'educational' skills from the process of guidance;
- receive structured support and feedback related to their guidance needs;

and encourage tutors to:

- rely less on themselves as the expert and giver of information, and more on their skills of enabling, advising, informing, counselling, reviewing, feeding back;
- create an opportunity for students to learn and gain new understanding from the process of guidance;
- assess whether their students' needs are being met;
- network with specialist colleagues.

If tutors can effectively employ their skills in support of the guidance process, then the tutorial can become a highly relevant and positive experience in which students can discuss and explore their guidance needs. For example, where supported self-study resources are used, the tutorial approach can allow aspects of the careers programme to be more closely tailored to individual needs and interests, thereby motivating students to engage actively in the process of learning and guidance.

Since effective guidance work is also dependent upon students developing relevant 'core' skills such as self-assessment, planning and reviewing, it adds strong support to the value of the tutorial as a key part of guidance provision, and therefore as an important context in which tutors and students can engage in careers work. Personal tutors have the benefit of regular contact with their students, which provides an opportunity to develop relationships of mutual understanding and trust. Given that the nature of careers guidance often involves personal disclosure, an effective and trusted tutor is well placed to create a climate for such dialogue, whether with individuals or small groups (HMI, 1992). The tutorial, therefore, offers a strongly supportive context for discussion about careers issues. It also provides a basis for utilising supported self-study methods to promote individual and group enquiry.

A further advantage of developing a tutor-based approach, is that it offers to enhance guidance provision without placing unreasonable demands upon the timetable, although it does place more burdens upon tutors and the time they have available. In practice, the capacity of tutors to give time to guidance is critical to the success of this approach.

What is Supported Self-study?

Supported self-study is not a new concept. The basic idea has been around for a long time although like other student-centred systems, it is more highly regarded in some quarters than in others. According to Waterhouse (1988), there are two key concepts – *support* and *self*.

If students are to be helped to *progressively* acquire the skills of the 'autonomous learner', they need *support*. This is seen in terms of:

- the support of careful and sensitive tutoring;
- the support of good management at all levels within the institution;
- the support of specially chosen learning resources.

Waterhouse claims that most efforts in education are concentrated on the presentation and delivery of knowledge and ideas, when instead, they should give much more attention to creating the right environment for learning and helping the learner to learn. Meaning, he says, does not belong to the knowledge we present but resides in the experience of the learner. So, finding ways of helping young people to discover personal meaning is the guiding principle of supported self-study. It is also central to the purposes of guidance.

How Does Supported Self-study Work?

The process of supported self-study can be described as a cycle involving three stages. Students have a tutorial, which is followed by a period of supported self-study, followed by a further tutorial. The tutorial is the essential element during which two things need to be done.

- *Stage 1 (tutorial phase)*. Tutors work with students to plan and negotiate what will be done within an agreed timescale. Tutors will also specify what support is available.
- *Stage 2 (supported or guided self-study phase)*. Students use selected self-study materials as a framework for their enquiry. Advice and tutor support should also be available during this phase, which in practice should not normally exceed two weeks before the review tutorial.
- *Stage 3 (tutorial phase)*. Tutors and students review what has been achieved and decide what may need to follow.

This approach advocates that the benefits of supported self-study can *only* work successfully if located within the tutorial cycle described and illustrated in Figure 5.1. Properly managed, the small group tutorial can provide students with an important and relatively secure context in which to explore their guidance needs.

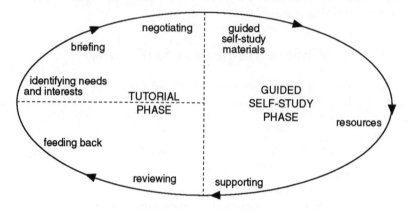

Figure 5.1 *Managing guidance through the tutorial cycle*

Developing this Approach in Schools and Colleges

For the past three years, a number of Kent schools and a college of further education have been engaged in an initiative aimed at implementing guidance work through their post-16 tutorial programme. The underlying premise of this initiative was that the supported self-study methodology can promote effective guidance work through the tutorial system and can therefore be used to enhance the school or college's contribution to raising standards in guidance. It was also based on the premise that if tutors and students were going to undertake guidance work in tutorials, they would need tailor-made materials, and a publication was devised for that purpose.

Relating this Approach to the Aims of CEG

The importance of high quality careers education and guidance has been widely documented in recent years (CBI, 1989, 1993a, 1993b; Jones, 1990; Killeen *et al* 1992; Watts, 1993, 1995). Young people need help to understand what they want and what they have to offer working life. They need to know how opportunity structures operate in a changing society and economy, and how these are accessed. Evaluating options, making weighty and informed decisions and coping with the implementation that ensues, are all heady responsibilities.

In helping students to achieve these outcomes, practitioners need to ensure that the range of guidance services on offer contribute to the wider educative process, and at the same time, recognise the needs of individual learning styles and preferences. Clearly, irrespective of the merits of any one approach, a range of learning strategies is required in addition to those described in this chapter (Killeen and Kidd, 1993). Account can be taken of how individuals differently approach the process of 'career planning', and this should inform the guidance help that tutors offer. An effective programme of post-16 guidance therefore needs to offer differentiation in provision, but this still must be grounded within a clear context of personal support.

Providers of guidance therefore have to be certain that what they offer will genuinely help students learn how to secure the knowledge and skills relevant to their decision-making needs. In re-examining the role of the tutorial and the associated (but not dependent) methodology of supported self-study, providers can explore and develop new strategies for creating an effective learning environment for guidance, in which to underpin their more established range of techniques.

The Role of Supported Self-study Materials

The role of supported self-study materials is to provide students with a framework for research. Well-constructed resources can provide something similar to a map that can help both students and tutors plan a guidance-related enquiry. Used in this way, this approach can offer a number of positive benefits for students by:

- helping both students and tutors to discuss and clarify aims and objectives;
- developing strategies to help students to make economic use of information resources;
- providing a number of sequential activities that are relevant to a particular 'guidance topic';
- offering sufficient material to engage the student with the essential issues;
- forming working documents, used to include and record learning;
- offering an aid to students in self-assessment and future planning – the very essence of effective tutorials.

In practice, there are different ways of implementing this approach, although each student should still be able to negotiate with their tutor which areas of support they need at any given time, and then, in conjunction with a tutorial, commence whichever enquiry is appropriate to their needs and interests. This can work well with small groups who share a common interest or concern. It also promotes peer support and review.

Guidance work through tutorials should be planned in conjunction with the overall careers programme. For example, if tutors know in advance that the careers tutor is organising a series of talks on higher education, post-16 tutors will be able to undertake preparatory and follow-up work with interested students through the tutorial cycle, using supported self-study resources as the framework for enquiry.

Margin Notes

i INTRODUCTION TO THIS GUIDE

Students often make a number of visits during their studies. These may be to employers or to universities and colleges and be made for a number of different purposes. These could include work placements as part of a course or a fact finding visit to a college. Either way, good preparation will be rewarded with better information, new insights and experiences, or even the offer of a job or college place. This Career Guide will help you get the most from such activities.

r RESOURCES

Listed below are resources which you may find useful to complete the activities in this guide. The reference number for each resource is highlighted in the margin e.g. **R9, R12.**

R9	Career Guide - Application Forms	KC&GS
R12	Career Guide - Completing an Application Form for HE	KC&GS
R16	Career Guide - Marketing Yourself	KC&GS
R17	Career Guide - Preparing A CV	KC&GS
R18	Career Guide - Preparing for interview	KC&GS
R65	MicroDOORS - Software	COIC
R69	Occupations	COIC
R74	Prospectuses, Adult Education	FE & HE
R76	The Natwest Student Book	Trotman

Other resources you may wish to use

p PLANNING YOUR WORK

The activities that follow are designed to help you cover the key areas described on the front page. You may not need to do them all. Read through the guide, and if necessary, discuss with your Tutor or Careers Adviser which activities would be most appropriate for you.

1 ACTIVITY: WHY I NEED TO MAKE VISITS?

Think about the particular course you are studying. Will it include visits to employers as part of the syllabus? Could this be for work experience or work shadowing? Maybe these things will be optional. What about visits to universities to find out more about their courses? How likely are you to make a visit of this sort?

Figure 5.2 *Preparing for a visit to university or an employer (Extract from one of a series of post-16 career guides published by Kent Careers and Guidance Service and Network Education Press. Reproduced with permission.)*

Margin Notes

Use the box below to help you identify the type of visits you may need to make during your present course of study.

Visits I shall need to make as part of my course	Visits I can choose to make which are not part of my course
What will be the purpose?	What will be the purpose?
When will these visits take place?	When will these visits take place?
Who will be responsible for organising them?	Who will be responsible for organising them?

2 ACTIVITY: VISITS TO EMPLOYERS

Work experience or work shadowing may be a compulsory or optional part of your course. These opportunities can be particularly valuable for further exploration of your career ideas.

Task 1

Use the diagram to list some of the ways in which you could benefit from visits to employers.

Work shadowing

BENEFITS

Task 2

If you are planning to visit an employer in the near future think about what you will want to find out. Use the grid and select the boxes relevant to your needs. You may want to construct your own chart in preparation for your visit.

Figure 5.2 *Preparing for a visit to university or an employer*

Margin Notes		
	I want/need to visit	**In order to**
	Employers who may be able to offer the type of help I want	
	Name/Address/Tel No.	**Name of Contact**
	How much time will I need to spend there? (This will depend on what you want to achieve and how much time both you and the employer have available).	
	When would be the best time to go? (for yourself and the employer)	
R65 **R69**	*What sort of things should I look for?*	
	What sort of information will the employer expect from me?	
	How do I prepare for a visit? Who do I need to liaise with in school/college?	
	What are my next steps?	

Finally, it is always important to review what happened after you have completed your visits or work placement. Normally this will be done with your tutors.

Figure 5.2 *Preparing for a visit to university or an employer*

Margin Notes

3 ACTIVITY: VISITS TO UNIVERSITIES OR COLLEGES

Students usually visit universities or colleges because they are interested to find out what they are like and whether it is the sort of place where they would wish to live and study. Sometimes these visits are organised by the university or college itself, such as open days, but it is also possible for students to arrange their own visits as well. Since the cost and time involved can be quite considerable, visits need to be carefully considered to ensure maximum value.

Task 1

What sort of information will you want to find out about a university or college? Use the table to set out your ideas.

Information about courses	Information about the department
Information about the institution and the neighbouring area	Information about student facilities
Information about accommodation	Information about travel costs
Other Categories (add your own)	

Figure 5.2 *Preparing for a visit to university or an employer*

Well-developed, supported, self-study materials should be used as a flexible tool, enabling students to select those parts of the resource that are appropriate to their needs. Resources should also be modified and supplemented in order to make them more relevant. Over time, these additional resources can be coordinated for inclusion in the careers resource area and copies made available to all tutors.

Preparing Tutors and Students for Using Supported Self-study Resources

Supported self-study resources are not a substitute for effective tutoring, but tutors will almost certainly benefit from having access to these materials. Well-constructed materials provide a basis for discussion and planning the enquiry. Evidence from work in Kent provided the following insights.

1. Resources will be most effective when used as part of a planned programme of guidance. Where this approach is used as a 'bolt-on' or as a substitute for a broader careers' entitlement it will not be satisfactory.
2. Resources can be used with individuals or groups. Probably a small group tutorial of five or six is ideal. While they do not require tutors to have any expertise in careers education, there may be a real advantage in the tutor introducing the topic on a class or group basis. Tutors also benefit from being able to invite the careers teacher or careers adviser to assist in introducing or reviewing a topic.
3. Tutorials must be participative. Students should be encouraged to do most of the thinking. Each tutorial should also have a clear agenda and a timescale for work agreed.
4. Students should want to use this approach as part of their own process of enquiry. Not all students will be familiar with this method of working, or immediately appreciate the value of a supported self-study approach to learning. Tutors need to explain this method to students and deal with any concerns. The relationship between this work and the broader careers programme also needs to be made clear.
5. This approach will not work without support. Some students will be able to work independently with minimal help, but the majority will not. The principle is *supported* self-study, not *self*-supported study. The follow-up tutorial is therefore particularly important in order to:
   - review students' progress and offer them feedback;
   - discuss whether these activities have helped meet their needs or whether further guidance and support is appropriate;
   - identify the next part of the guidance process, including referral.

This approach also emphasises the importance of effective tutoring in helping students to make important *connections* between a wide range of learning activities, life experiences, roles and relationships, and to appreciate the relevance that these have to future career/educational choice (Whiteside, 1994, p.391). Students should be encouraged to look for connective ideas and feedback, not only through the formal curriculum, but also through their participation and experience of extra-curricular activities that can equally inform their career planning.

Management Issues

Creating the right climate for the introduction of supported self-study is an important first step. Gaining the support and commitment of both management and tutors will be crucial to its success. Proposals to implement such an approach may want to address the following questions.

- How does the supported self-study process relate to the school/college development plan?
- How will post-16 tutors be persuaded to take part?
- How will staff training be managed?
- How will this approach support and enhance existing guidance provision?
- How can it enhance action planning and recording achievement?
- How can it support other curricular programmes?
- How will it be funded and resourced?

A report or proposal may also want to outline a summary of the potential benefits for the institution:

- it makes the progress of the individual student the focus for institutional, curriculum and staff development;
- it means that work and resources are firmly centred on the student;
- it allows for a differentiated approach to student learning;
- it enables both students and tutors to derive more value from the tutorial;
- students are likely to be better motivated to research their interests and place more value on the guidance process;
- students are developing personal and study skills with broad curricular relevance.

Implementation Issues

Programme planning will be necessary in order to agree how the supported self-study materials will be used in support of the tutorial process. Relating the use of the tutorial to the existing careers programme is essential. The tutorial approach is supplementary to the main careers programme, not a replacement for it. The planning schedule in Figure 5.3 could be used for this purpose.

MODULE/UNIT/THEME

1. What knowledge, skills and understanding do we want students to have achieved as a result of following this module/unit/theme?

   Knowledge of. . .   Able to. . .   Understand. . .

   •   •   •

   •   •   •

   •   •   •

2. What range of learning activities can we provide/facilitate in support of the above?

   (a) Those already present within the curriculum

   (b) Those which require additional provision

   (c) The role which supported self-study materials can play in supporting this process

3. How can we best manage these activities and ensure that they provide students with a positive experience of learning?

   •

   •

   •

Figure 5.3 *Example of a programme planning schedule*

Tutors will need adequate training and support. They will need to be comfortable with the workings of the guidance management cycle, especially the review phase. A basic familiarity with the careers library is also important. Students will need proper preparation for this method of working. Monitoring and evaluation will provide you with useful feedback since this is a process that will need developing and some fine tuning.

Summary and Conclusion

In this chapter I have tried to demonstrate that current policy initiatives, aimed at improving the quality of guidance provision for post-16 students, will benefit from providers taking a fresh look at how existing teaching and learning structures can be modified or developed to enable tutors and students to engage effectively in the guidance process. It has been argued that the tutorial can provide valuable scope for enhancing guidance work, and that supported self-study methods are well suited to encouraging individual and peer group enquiry within this particular learning context.

Viewing guidance as an additional and non-mainstream activity is unlikely to create the improvements that policy makers are looking for, and that both staff and students need. The management of guidance as an intrinsic part of student programmes requires sophisticated but practical strategies to allow curriculum managers, teachers, tutors and careers practitioners to negotiate and network together in partnership. Making optimum use of existing systems provides an important first step in that process.

CHAPTER 6

CAREERS EDUCATION AND GUIDANCE AND SPECIAL EDUCATIONAL NEEDS

Christine Thomas

Managing the transition from school to the next life stage is a challenge for all young people, but for those with special educational needs it can be traumatic and disorienting. In this chapter I will argue that careers education and guidance (CEG) has a crucial and central role to play in the developing lives of students with special needs. Furthermore, the way in which students learn about 'careers' will be explored in terms of specific learning objectives. This will be complemented by a description of some delivery mechanisms that can be used to address such objectives. Careers programmes must use a student-centred approach, which is both flexible and individualised, if students are to exercise their right to knowledge about the world outside school. In concluding, some suggested ways forward, for special schools and those working with special educational needs (SEN) students in mainstream schools, will be offered.

Space does not permit a detailed definition of 'special educational needs'. However, within this chapter it refers to either students in special schools (eg, physical disability, sensory impairment, emotional and behavioural behaviour or moderate learning difficulties) or those students in mainstream schools who have a statement of special need. More precise definitions and details can be obtained from the Education Act and Code of Practice (1993).

The Importance of CEG for SEN Students

One of the aims of the 1988 Education Reform Act was to 'prepare pupils for the opportunities, experiences and responsibilities of adult life'. Clearly CEG is central to this preparation and 'career' should be viewed in its broadest sense, as one's path through life including a wide range of possible activities such as work, training, education, parenthood, sheltered programmes and unemployment. Many students with special needs, but particularly those with the most severe learning difficulties, may never enter into formal employment or training. Nonetheless, these students have the right to find out about the world around them, including the world of work, education and training, as part of their general education programme. Indeed, many SEN students have led very sheltered lives and have been protected, understandably, from the outside world. For example, students who attend special schools are often transported to and from the school by a special bus and do not mix with students other than their immediate peers. Many will have little contact with the varied occupational structures that can be more easily experienced by their 'mainstream' contemporaries in social contexts, such as shopping on a Saturday, playing sport or having a part-time job. From this viewpoint, a broad and imaginative careers and lifeskills programme is crucial.

Also, many students with learning difficulties are not able to use more formal information on progression routes, such as college leaflets, careers books and guides and leaflets produced by outside agencies, which are widely available to the general public. Thus careers programmes must look to providing information in an accessible form.

Learning Objectives

Law and Watts (1977) provide a useful framework of learning objectives for careers education and guidance:

- decision-making skills;
- opportunity awareness;
- transition skills;
- self-awareness.

Each of these areas provides a challenge for students with special needs. For example, everyday decisions are often made by others on behalf of students who therefore have little, if any, experience of practising this transferable skill in non-career based contexts. A similar lack of experience may well impede their ability to cope with transitions. It is quite common for special schools to cater for children as young as three years of age and as old as 19, thus preventing any palpable transition. Students' awareness of the opportunities of the adult world can be limited as described above, in addition to the sometimes narrow spectrum of choices perceived by parents.

Self-awareness is a difficult concept to tackle in any careers programme, but is particularly fraught with difficulties in a special needs setting. Students develop their self-image from a wide range of external stimuli, including their families, their particular needs, the way in which they are treated by others and their experience of success and failure in life so far. Bevan (1995) describes this difference in how we view ourselves in the world as our 'personal construct theory'. In other words we all construct a different view of events and situations and therefore hold different opinions about them. Students with special needs may well have very inappropriate constructs of themselves, perhaps refusing to believe that they could possibly succeed at college, when in fact they might do so with some confidence boosting. Conversely, students may continue to hold quite unrealistic expectations for themselves long after their mainstream peers have passed this 'fantasy' stage in their thinking about careers.

A Student-centred Approach

Learning about careers and progression while at school, is learning out of context. Countless learning theorists have argued that students learn most effectively by experiencing new ideas directly. Barnes (1989), for example, stresses the gulf between the de-contextualised knowledge processed in schools and the way in which new skills and ideas are acquired in everyday living. He advocates a curriculum based on the problem solving of relevant topics, in order for students to conceptualise and construct understandings. Whitehead (1989), similarly supports the need for experiential learning that leads to the mastery of skills.

Learning by doing is central to an effective careers programme for students with special needs. Much of the learning is abstract and distant from students' current lives. Only by direct experience are students able to build on or 'scaffold' (Wood, 1988) their existing knowledge or, indeed, alter their perceptions of the world beyond school.

Careers learning should also be student-centred in its individualised approach. As each student has different needs, so individualised programmes must be developed with close one-to-one monitoring and review. This is aided by the annual review cycle mandatory for statemented students and the requirement that a careers adviser be invited to 14+ reviews.

In order to reflect the many different ways in which students learn and respond, a variety of teaching and learning strategies should be employed. Students are more likely to be motivated by a varied diet of activities, coordinated centrally to form a coherent programme. Such a model for a careers curriculum would necessitate very careful planning and documentation, in order to ensure progression between learning objectives and key stages. A useful resource for using this model can be found in *Planning a Student Centred Approach to Careers Education*, (Birmingham Careers Service, 1990).

Delivery Mechanisms

A wide repertoire of activities has been used by schools, in order to support learning about careers. The following case studies are taken from special schools in the London boroughs of Hackney and Islington, who are part of the year 9/10 careers project. Each example constitutes one way of addressing some or all of the four learning objectives referred to earlier.

- The use of *role models* in a school for students with physical disabilities. This has widened the students' awareness of higher level occupations and encouraged the more academically able to aim high.
- A *mini-enterprise* that runs every week as part of students' normal curriculum in a severe learning difficulties school. The sixth form students run a snack business one day per week, which involves team work, collecting orders, buying and preparing food, packaging, pricing and delivering.
- A series of *work-related visits* to depict a range of occupational areas such as health, manufacturing, protective services and plants, animals and the land. Autistic students have complete records of the visits using computer software.
- An *industry week* for emotional and behavioural difficulties/mild learning difficulties students from years 10 and 11. This involved visits to places of work, interviewing people about their jobs, workshops for different occupational areas and preparation for work experience.
- *Short work experience* placements for a range of students. Some attend the same workplace for one afternoon per week, some attend with a carer and others are in sheltered placements for two or three days at a time.
- *Computer-assisted learning* such as using CID (Careers Information Database), produced by 'Careersoft' with EBD (educational and behavioural difficulties) students. Wordprocessing CVs and statements for the NRA (National Record of Achievement). Using scanners and computer-linked cameras to illustrate students work.
- *Individual action planning* for all students linked to annual reviews and careers interviews, often using computer software.
- *Travel training* for all students, to help them become more able to find their way to a given location. Others to travel on public transport with a helper.
- *Simulated decision making* for EBD students, involving a local company, giving the students a real situation to solve.
- *College links* for all students, in order to sample college life by attending regularly. For example, one day per fortnight to join in a course and mix with other students.

Ways Forward

In developing a student-centred approach to careers education and guidance, examples of delivery mechanisms cited are not intended to be comprehensive, but rather to give a flavour of some of the imaginative ways in which schools are focusing on the individual needs of students. Throughout all of the case studies, key principles are embedded. First, the activities are open to all students irrespective of their ability to enter the world of employment, training or further education. Secondly, each experience is evaluated, reviewed and recorded by students. A portfolio of students work is kept to enhance the NRA. Finally, each activity in a school is only seen as part of a range of learning opportunities, which constitutes the whole programme of CEG. Through careful planning progression can be plotted.

Schools wishing to develop their careers programme for students with special needs would benefit from the following sorts of activities.

- Talking to colleagues from other similar schools. In particular, events may be easier to organise in collaboration with another school given the small number of students involved.
- Involving the Careers Service in developmental discussions. Careers advisers often have access to suitable contacts for visits and so on.
- Talking to the students themselves and their parents. Many students are aware of the sort of help that they need and the way in which they learn most effectively.
- Brainstorming the learning needs of students in relation to careers education and guidance. Once these are agreed, schools can analyse current provision against them.
- Keeping up to date with special needs resources such as videos, curriculum packs and computer software. Again, the Careers Service should be able to help.
- Using the planning and reviewing systems in the school. Careers work should be regularly evaluated and development work recorded as part of the school development plan.

In focusing on an appropriate programme of careers work for students with special needs, attention is brought to the learning needs of all students. All of our young people are individuals, with varied needs. Each sees the world and her/his place in it uniquely and each learns in a slightly different way. Thus, in providing a learning context for students with special needs, a relevant and stimulating careers curriculum is possible for all.

CHAPTER 7

THE CAREERS EDUCATION CURRICULUM: THE 'EDUCATION FOR CHOICE' PROJECT

Andrew Edwards and Jean-Luc Mure with Greg Robb

This chapter describes the first phase of a curriculum project set up in 1994 by Kent Careers and Guidance Service (KCGS) in collaboration with 11 secondary schools. The aim of the project was to adapt and pilot an 'experiential' careers education and guidance programme originally developed in Quebec, where it still forms part of the statutory curriculum, and which was subsequently adapted in France by the Association Trouver/Créer. The project was launched under the direction of Andrew Edwards (then Development Manager with KCGS). Jean-Luc Mure, Vice President of the Association Trouver/Créer, provided consultancy and support with training. Greg Robb, as Head of Careers in one of the schools involved in the pilot project, provides a case study at the end of the chapter.

Why Education for Choice?

In North America and Europe, the changing social and economic context has led to changes in guidance practice, the challenge has been on two fronts: the transformation of the social and economic world and the changing status of men and women. Three factors in particular, impinge upon the guidance process.

1. Our social and economic environment is changing more and more rapidly due to the progress made by science and technology in recent years, and at the same time, work is becoming both more complex and uncertain.
2. This development has brought about profound changes in people's relationships at work, in their social and professional lives, in the

knowledge and images that they have about the employment market and in their information and communication networks.
3. Today, people are seen as actors in their own lives. Paradoxically, we must increasingly become more autonomous and responsible for our own career development, since society finds it more and more difficult to provide economic opportunities and social structures that help individuals to feel part of the community.

Faced with this socio-economic transformation, guidance can no longer be seen simply as a process of information giving where the aim is to match 'the right person with the right job'. In a social and professional world that is becoming increasingly difficult to assess and predict, it is no longer possible to give individuals information on a 'once and for all' basis that will set them up for life. Guidance must now be concerned with helping adults and young people to develop their plans and ideas for future training and to be able to relate these to their social and vocational needs. This process should take place gradually, all the while providing them with the means to become more informed, to explore the social and economic environment and to know themselves better. People need a methodology rather than just information.

Guidance can be defined as a developmental process that continues throughout adolescence and the whole of life, during which individuals explore and then implement educational, social and vocational plans. The careers programme is therefore not based merely on information-giving but on experiential learning to help students to make choices, understand effective decision-making and plan their career. Further, by reconciling hopes and aspirations with reality, students move to new levels of maturity. If finding one's direction in life requires time and skill, then perhaps this is a skill that can be learnt. Education, particularly secondary education, can play an important role in helping young people to develop and explore their plans for the future. With this in mind, three researchers from Quebec, Pelletier, Noiseux and Bujold, put forward a methodology, Activation of Vocational and Personal Development (ADVP), for constructing educational guidance programmes. In Quebec, this curriculum programme was subsequently renamed 'Career Choice Education'. The French adaptation that followed in the late 1980s was entitled 'Education for Choice' (EC).

What is Education for Choice?

This is an educational programme for use in secondary schools that aims to enable young people to make more satisfying choices through acquiring new skills and knowledge and by developing positive attitudes. The programme aims to enable students to gain greater self-awareness, a greater understanding of their environment and to learn methods and strategies for planning their future. The programme is built around a number of teaching sessions that aim to give students the tools to determine their own future. These are structured around four principal stages.

- The first stage engages students in an *exploration process* by working through a range of **experiences**. These varied experiences will further the construction of a richer self-identity through new perceptions and information gathered about school, work and themselves.
- In the second stage students are encouraged to *process and exploit their experiences*, to **crystallise** (or conceptualise) them. The information collected should be classified and organised into groups or concepts, such as self and environment.
- Students must then be allowed to *consolidate their experiences*, to give them meaning, to define new needs. They need to reflect upon their values, to compare and evaluate them so that they are able to make a choice. This is the **specification** stage and its ultimate aim, through the joint operation of comparing and evaluating, is to arrive at an informed and satisfactory choice, the 'birth' of a plan for the future.
- The final stage, **realisation** (putting the plan into action), is meant to encourage young people to take responsibility for their choices, to anticipate future action, to think of alternative strategies and finally, in order to make further progress, to begin the process of exploration again.

The Quebec programme has been in use in schools since 1985 and the EC (Education des Choix) programme was adapted in France in 1988 by a team of careers advisers, all trainers and members of the Association (Trouver/Créer). It was piloted from 1988 onwards in a number of secondary schools with students from 11 to 15 years old. The pilot took place in several regions but was mainly confined to the Rhone-Alps area (Grenoble, Lyon). Teams of teachers and careers advisers were trained by officers from the Trouver/Créer Association, often within the framework of the National Education System.

In November 1994, a team from this association, under the leadership of Robert Solazzi, completely revised EC and brought out a new programme, 'Education for Choice: Learning To Find Our Way In Life'. This programme responds more appropriately to French and European issues on guidance and has taken into account the lessons learnt from the evaluation studies.

Preliminary Findings from the Implementation of EC in France

The EC programme covers the first four years of secondary education and offers students approximately 15 sessions each lasting one hour. These sessions are usually taught by the teacher, sometimes with the help of a careers adviser. After the first experimental phase, the impact has been significant but varies from region to region. Although EC is based on a new concept of guidance, it still complies with the demands of the National Curriculum in France. This requires that guidance should continue throughout a student's education and should be a continuous process of constructing and consolidating plans for vocational training. EC will gradually be introduced in a variety of different ways throughout the various educational regions of France.

Several local evaluation studies were undertaken in order to identify the effects that the implementation of EC has had on secondary schools. As an example, we can take the results of the evaluation carried out in a secondary school in the suburbs of Grenoble. This school has been working with the programme since 1988 and its year 10 students completed the full four-year programme in June 1994. The students mainly come from underprivileged backgrounds and 27 per cent of the school population consists of students from ethnic minorities. The evaluation was carried out jointly by researchers from Trouver/Créer and from INOP (National Institute of Vocational Guidance in Paris). This was undertaken at the request of the Regional Council of the Ile de France who were keen to discover how effective the method was before promoting it to other educational districts such as Paris, Creteil and Versailles. The INOP researchers were interested in the psychological effects of the methodology on students and in particular their level of vocational maturity. Their findings were as follows:

'Generally the approach was well received by young people. . . . It is clearly showing positive effects on vocational maturity (at least on self-awareness and awareness of training opportunities) and seems to have been of greater benefit to boys.'

The researchers from Trouver/Créer were more interested in the way the methodology had been put into practice, both from the point of view of the students and parents as well as that of the teachers, headteachers and career advisers. They concluded:

'For the majority of people questioned, the different objectives were achieved. Some of the results can be measured in a tangible way: no more problems with what to do at the end of Year 10, an overall increase in school results and significant increase in passes of the 'Brevet' (exam taken at the end of secondary education). . . . It was also noticed that teamwork had improved and the school benefited from better internal organisation. . . . On the other hand it was felt that parents could be more involved.

'In conclusion, the results relating to the level of guidance given to students, the effect on the general working atmosphere in the school, the time given for advance preparation rather than seeing the guidance process as an emergency procedure, all of these elements demonstrate the effectiveness of the EC methodology. The main factors behind these results were the head-teachers, supporting and encouraging the project, the team of well trained teachers, the guidance centre and careers advisers, the administration and local communities who supported the EC project.'

These encouraging results show that it is worth continuing with the work started in France, and that as many secondary students as possible (and also university students and young adults) should be provided with the means to construct and implement their plans and ideas for the future.

Adapting 'Education for Choice'

During the early 1990s, Kent Careers and Guidance Service (KCGS) began to review and rethink its philosophy and approach to guidance. While it was recognised that individual guidance was always going to be important, careers advisers were well aware that unless students had been properly prepared for making 'informed and realistic' decisions about their future lives, the benefits of individual guidance are often minimised. Since the context for such learning in schools is primarily through the curriculum, it was increasingly evident that careers advisers work with individuals could be much improved if the content and quality of careers education could be raised to promote the knowledge, skills and understanding students needed.

Exposure through PETRA (see glossary, page 161) to the ideas and practices of other European practitioners also had an impact on thinking. Of particular interest was the discovery of how French and Canadian academics and practitioners had developed a careers education curriculum for the secondary age range based upon experiential approaches to teaching and learning connected to developmental theories of career development. Links were subsequently formed with the Trouver/Créer Association, which facilitated exchange visits and training. It was soon recognised that a number of key features from the Canadian and French programmes were highly relevant to our own situation:

- the curriculum programme emphasises student participation – learning by doing;
- student needs and aspirations are recognised;
- students will learn that choosing a career is something to be experienced rather than an academic exercise;
- teachers have a methodology and support materials that give coherence and interest to the careers education process;
- teachers can enjoy the benefit of teaching through student self-discovery;
- the ultimate aim is to make students aware that they are responsible for their own professional and personal identities and to help them to acquire the skills to realise their ambitions.

Establishing the Project

The rationale for setting up a new curriculum project was derived from some of the internal factors referred to earlier, as well as an anticipation of a series of government funding initiatives to support the training of teachers and improved guidance for students. Central to this project, however, was the recognition by the Careers Service of its potential to exercise a strategic role in facilitating a new curriculum initiative while using its transnational network in the process. The 'coincidence' of these factors was underpinned by a conviction borne from our experience with schools that while the curriculum remained a major and influential context for undertaking careers work with students, it was still largely unsupported and underdeveloped. A project was therefore finally established between the Careers Service and 11 schools with the objectives of developing:

- a strategic partnership between schools, TVEI, the Careers Service, French and Canadian partners and an HEI, which can establish common ownership and commitment to the principles of good practice;
- a curriculum that is up-to-date and relevant to the needs of young people in the second half of the 1990s;
- a curriculum that addresses the process of effective teaching and learning and that demonstrably raises standards of student learning;
- a curriculum based upon methodologies designed to facilitate vocational development;
- a curriculum that raises self-esteem, motivation and interest;
- a process that increases the skill, interest and motivation of all teachers associated with careers work;
- a methodology that facilitates a teacher-researcher model of curriculum development.

Following initial countywide consultation meetings, nearly 60 schools expressed an interest in taking part. The 18-month pilot project was therefore divided into three phases, with a 'first intake' of 11 schools. Immediate action required a business plan to be drafted for the 18-month pilot project, followed by:

- briefing meetings for teachers;
- joint training in curriculum methodology for teachers and careers advisers;
- joint training for other teachers organised and delivered by teachers and careers advisers;
- adaptation and piloting process;
- joint monitoring and evaluation by teachers and careers advisers.

Training

Training for this work was undertaken by Jean-Luc Mure (Trouver/Créer), Andrew Edwards (then Development Manager with KCGS) and David Frost (Canterbury Christ Church College). Each phase received two days introductory training, and both courses were attended by careers teachers, careers advisers and their team managers. Following this initial training, each school was asked to host a training session for their own colleagues who were going to be associated with the programme. This session was usually planned and conducted by both the careers teacher and careers adviser. A variety of staff were invited – year 9 tutors, year heads, other year group tutors and headteachers. Some schools arranged for this training to take place off school premises either during school hours or in the evening. In general, off-site sessions were very successful. Most included an experiential activity, as a means of introducing colleagues to the teaching approach of Education for Choice.

Staff reactions to these sessions varied. In some schools, all Year 9 form tutors were expected to deliver the programme as part of the personal and social education (PSE) programme. Although the majority of tutors were enthusiastic, it was reported that some tutors, already ambivalent about their PSE role, were less receptive to the programme. For others, the teacher guides provided valuable and much needed resources. In schools where tutors had chosen to teach PSE, the response was very positive. Once the schools began delivering the programme, some careers teachers organised regular meetings for the staff involved. These meetings were held weekly in some schools, and on a more ad hoc basis in others. Staff used this time to:

- give feedback and evaluate the materials;
- share student feedback and responses to the lessons;
- raise issues and areas of concern;
- discuss the delivery of subsequent units.

These meetings, particularly when held on a regular basis, were an important factor in the determining the overall success of the programme. Further training events were also organised for careers teachers and careers advisers, providing an opportunity to review the classroom materials and consider appropriate teaching methods.

Programme Delivery

The context in which the programme was delivered varied in each school, although it was primarily aimed at supporting teachers who were required to deliver CEG through discrete periods, PSE or personal tutorial time. Aspects of the programme also demonstrated the wider relevance of other curriculum subjects to CEG, and placed strong emphasis on developing students' interpersonal skills.

The materials were designed to last for at least a 45-minute period. The first module was aimed at year 9 students and dealt in detail with the theme of personal identity and self-appraisal, preparing the ground for year 10 option choice. Where schools had sufficient time available, the programme ran smoothly. In other instances, problems were encountered where the length of the tutorial period was too short to give adequate coverage to the themes involved. Some schools creatively found time from other curriculum areas. Each student was also provided with a purpose designed portfolio in which to store their curriculum materials. This feature did much to raise the status of the programme so far as the students were concerned. It was also appreciated by tutors.

Evaluation

Careers teachers were asked to monitor and evaluate the progress and development of the project within their own schools. Guidelines on evaluation methods were given for this purpose. At the end of the first phase of the pilot (March, 1995), each careers teacher was asked to give a short presentation to other members of the project group and to provide a short evaluation report outlining their experiences to date. Each school was also visited by the project manager to review progress and discuss matters arising from the project. Some classroom observation was also undertaken. Issues arising included:

- curriculum materials – language and concepts;
- curriculum time;
- the implications for classroom management;
- student interest and understanding;
- learning outcomes for students;
- staff reaction;
- training needs;
- organisation and management of the programme;
- parental interest and reaction.

Careers teachers and careers advisers cooperated in monitoring and evaluating the progress of the programme. Various techniques were used to gather information:

- student questionnaires;
- classroom diary;
- observation;
- staff questionnaires;
- staff meetings;
- informal discussions;
- parents' evenings;
- careers conventions.

Student Feedback

Overall, the response from students has been positive and enthusiastic. Students liked the discussions and enjoyed participating in the activities. Several schools included verbatim remarks from individual students.

> 'I think it was good because they let you do things yourself instead of doing it themselves.'

'It's different from any other work I've done. It's easy to understand, the ideas are a bit out of the ordinary.'

'I found that the wording of the project was very simple to follow and that the picture and writing size were clear and easy to see.'

Why did you like this?

'Because you can use your imagination. It was fun most of the time, but only because we talked about it.'

'A trip through life. More exciting than reading and writing.'

At times, some students found it difficult to make the links between the imaginary experiences and the objectives; these students didn't take quite so well to some of the units. Other students had difficulty putting their ideas into words or in dealing with some of the concepts involved. The level of language also proved difficult for some students. Where this was the case, teachers tended to re-phrase ideas and concepts in more familiar terms. Other teachers regarded the level of language as challenging, but not too difficult. Given the wide ability range of pupils involved, it was always going to be a difficult task to achieve a level of language that would be accessible to all.

Staff Feedback

Success in the project would also depend upon how the programme would be viewed by the teaching staff concerned. Some careers teachers reported that a small number of colleagues remained disinterested in teaching the programme, whereas others had developed a much more positive attitude based upon their experiences and student feedback. Many tutors welcomed having good quality teaching materials that were progressive and student centred in their approach.

The involvement of careers advisers in occasionally providing classroom support, was also appreciated by teaching staff. Careers advisers reported that their participation in the programme had helped to develop their relationship with students much earlier. It also encouraged a closer working relationship with other teachers. Most schools also saw the educational philosophy of 'Education for Choice' as congruent with their own. Other outcomes for students were also identified by teachers.

'It showed that students had been made to think and consider what was important to them.'

'Pupils have felt that they have been valued, that their opinions count.'

'Students – quite interested really, they love to talk around things, but putting things on paper is not their forte.'

'Awareness and use of information in the careers library has been increased greatly for year 9 students.'

Careers teachers also noted how the project had impacted upon their own colleagues.

> 'Year 9 tutors have, in the main, been positively affected by involvement in this work.'

> 'Raised awareness among group tutors in particular and has allowed them to make a more positive contribution to option choices.'

> 'Tutors have felt more confident in teaching careers within the PSE programme.'

Senior managers in schools were generally very supportive and enthusiastic, which was always going to be a key factor in determining the project's progress. Likewise, response from parents was very positive. A number of schools held year 9 parents' evenings which generated a great deal of interest in the programme. Two schools reported:

> 'Best ever year 9 parents' evening.'

> 'I have spoken to ten families tonight at the year 9 parents' evening and they were very positive about Education for Choice.'

Outcomes for Individuals

At the end of the first phase of the pilot (March, 1995), not all schools had finished the programme. Collectively however, they have produced evidence to suggest the following learning outcomes have been achieved.

- Increased students' awareness and understanding of careers.
- Improved decision-making skills which have been very noticeable at option choice.
- Students have taken pride in their work.
- Students have become more questioning – about themselves, their future needs and opportunities.
- Students have made substantially more use of the careers library.
- Students have been more responsive in their careers interviews.

Outcomes for Schools

In broad terms, these can be summarised as an increased profile for careers education and guidance, enhanced tutor skills and involvement in careers education, and strengthened links with the Careers Service.

> 'Careers education and guidance has always had a high profile – this has helped to embed it further down the school – and importantly, helped to identify and implement a student entitlement to CEG.'

> 'It has raised awareness of CEG, which had been tremendous.'

'It has certainly enhanced previous practice in Year 9 work and will form an important part of future programmes, particularly including greater involvement of group tutors.'

Case Study – Sir William Nottidge Technology School

(Greg Robb, Careers and Industry Manager)
This perspective is derived from my own personal experience of 18 years of careers work in schools, and based upon a commitment to careers education and guidance as a essential element in improving the overall quality of learning for our students. As such, I believe that CEG can be positioned so that it becomes more focused as an entitlement and central to the empowerment of future generations of students progressing through our schools and colleges.

I look back to *Working Together for a Better Future*, (DES/DE/Welsh Office, 1987) as a welcome benchmark in the development of careers education and guidance, and the subsequent publication of *Curriculum Matters 10* (DES/HMI, 1988), which offered a positive statement of what schools should be providing for their students. The fortunes of careers work in the intervening years are well documented elsewhere (see Chapter 1), but one of my major concerns has been that despite the strong support from the CBI and others, the ongoing uncertainty surrounding the place of CEG in the curriculum has continued, largely due to its non-statutory status. In my view, this has been amply illustrated by the insubstantial attention given to CEG through the OFSTED process.

More recently, the Dearing 'back to the drawing board' review has offered a further opportunity to flag up careers education. This pointed to the potential of 'freed up time' being available for careers. At the same time, it seemed to suggest the abandonment of the cross-curriculum themes. Where was careers to be? As in 1988 the possibility of careers education being integrated into a clearly coherent curriculum looked like being lost. Careers practitioners had to wait for the *Competitiveness, Helping Business to Win* White Paper (DTI, 1994) and an announcement from the Employment Department to provide funding for years 9 and 10 through the Training and Enterprise Councils (TECs). This funding was significant because, certainly in Kent, the TEC and Careers Service were able to fund audits to establish base lines for CEG provision in the county. Through an enhanced service level agreement (SLA), careers advisers were able to work with year 9 and 10 groups which raised the profile of individual unbiased counselling in schools. Importantly, it not only raised the status of careers advisers in schools, but it also introduced teachers to the range of progression opportunities, as well as their students. Short development projects were also funded which were managed by the Careers Service and served to enhance the status of careers education in schools.

However, the significant factor for my school was our involvement in the curriculum project described earlier in this chapter. This presented us with a very important opportunity because the school wished to develop a relevant curriculum to match its technological ethos. We saw this as a means of improving our performance in raising students' expectations and achievements. We were also keen to replace our existing careers programme, which although it met the demands of the National Curriculum, nonetheless reflected a traditional content dominated approach. The project also helped us to develop a curriculum entitlement and to involve form tutors actively in delivering the programme.

A major aim of the programme was to take year 9 and 10 students through a clear process, developing skills in self-awareness and decision making. Most importantly the ethos and rationale were clearly presented so that the tutors involved understood the curriculum methodology as well as the aims and objectives of each session. Staff also enjoyed the extra involvement and experience that the careers adviser brought to the process. It was evident from an early stage of the programme that it was highly effective in motivating students. The impact this made on students' use of the school careers library was a good performance indicator. So too, was the positive response of parents attending an options evening. Importantly, the tutors also felt happy working with a clearly written set of activities. Although further differentiation was required for some of the vocabulary, the learning outcomes were considerable for all students at a range of ability levels. A similar response is being voiced by the year 10 tutor team, which is delivering the programme at the time of writing. Regular review meetings have allowed the staff involved to share ideas and concerns and offer feedback on students' responses to the activities.

Careers education and guidance must address the developmental and learning needs of students, which is one of the chief objectives of this programme. In so doing, recognition needs to be given to the fact that an entitlement to careers can support the process of learning within a wider whole school curriculum entitlement.

Conclusion

This curriculum project in Kent is still in its early stages, and is currently in the process of being restructured to fit the change in circumstances that has taken place since it began in 1994. Essential to the ongoing development is the continued existence of a network of partners who remain committed to completing the process of adaptation, piloting, evaluation and revision. Equal attention has to be paid to training and support for tutors as well as the curriculum development itself. Structures are needed that facilitate support, liaison and feedback among the members of the project group as well as with external partners overseas. The 'new' context for this development will take the form of a small action research group which we feel is the model best suited to the task in hand, and very similar to that which has successfully operated in France for the past seven years.

CHAPTER 8

USING COMPUTERS IN CAREERS EDUCATION AND GUIDANCE

Marcus Offer

Computers have been used to provide resources for guidance since the late 1960s. For the first decade or so, the field was dominated by large mainframe computers and by systems such as CASCAID (Careers Advisory Service Computer Aid), devised by Leicestershire Careers Service. By the end of the 1970s, CASCAID had been joined by the JIIG-CAL (Job Ideas and Information Generator, Computer-assisted Learning) system from Edinburgh University.

Impact of the PC

In the 1980s, the arrival of the microcomputer, sitting on a desktop, meant that new, more interactive, ways of using the computer became possible. Now the client or student could input their details, their interests and their aspirations directly at the keyboard and get more or less instant feedback and reports. This type of computer program clearly had implications for the way guidance was delivered and for the processes of careers education. It seemed that individual students and clients of guidance might be able, for the first time, to 'help themselves' to guidance, in a way that reflected the high value given in the early and mid-80s to experiential learning and the empowering of autonomous learners. The number of games and simulations available on computer that enabled young people to try out what it was like to be, for example, manager of a supermarket or hotel, or to run a factory or a football club, reflected this trend. However, because many of these programs were written for the BBC computers, that were all the rage then in school computing, most are now no longer available for the PC-compatible hardware that took over in the late 1980s. Yet games and simulations are some of the most creative ways in which computers can be used to support learning, and the future development of virtual reality systems offers enormous possibilities for 'safe' experiences of new situations, in which people can try themselves out before making a real-world decision.

Information Management

There are many other ways of using the computer. Information management and retrieval has been one of the most obvious. We are not thinking, here, about the administrative and placing functions supported by computer, such as the Careers Service systems, used for holding information about local businesses, their vacancies, and about guidance clients, and matching the people to the vacancies. Computer-assisted guidance systems (CAGS) are about guidance: they offer to do some of what advisers did in the past. Computers are good at doing certain things that are more difficult for human beings. A good example is storing information about many thousands of courses and displaying quickly those bits of the information that are relevant to an individual's expressed needs. Computers can not only do this more reliably and objectively than human beings, but can empower the individual user by giving him or her more or less instant access to information resources that might have taken hours of expert time to assemble otherwise.

Matching People to Opportunities

Self-awareness and opportunity awareness are two of the four traditional aims of careers education and guidance, and the relationship between them is all-important. A link must be established between who I am, what I want and can offer, and the world of work. Another popular group of programs provides such a link. These offer some kind of self-assessment, whether a psychometric test or simply a checklist of ideas to work through, and then match the answers to a database of occupations or courses described in similar terms. Provided we can find common ways of describing the demands of jobs and the characteristics of individuals, such matching can fit square pegs to square holes with some success. Computers are good at doing the necessary donkey work required to compare one's declared profile to all the options at high speed and offering a rank-ordered list of options. This should be based on a more or less elaborate algorithm, which takes into account all the pluses and minuses, as opposed to the simple Yes/No logic and limited number of criteria used in most information retrieval systems. Such a process comes a lot closer to what most people understand by guidance.

Supporting Decision Making

Career choice, however, also requires decision making. There comes a point when you have to decide which of a number of presented possibilities you are going to plump for. When people experience difficulty at this stage, a computer program can model a rational process through which the pros and cons of such alternatives can be weighed. Such programs are usually content-free and focus on helping you analyse the factors you want to use in decision-making, and to apply these to a typical decision. They also offer the guidance worker or teacher a choice – is the objective to deliver a final decision for the individual, or to teach them a rational procedure through which future decisions can be made as well? At the same time, the very rationality of the model throws into relief the 'irrationality' of many human choice processes, and may raise issues for some individuals at a superordinate level that can only be dealt with by human counselling. 'Aye, there's the rub. . .'

Practical Tasks

Having made a decision, there is action to be taken and supported. Often this will be an application for a job or course and here dedicated wordprocessors have a role, usually with a tutorial program that will prompt you through the process of completing a curriculum vitae, writing letters of application or filling in forms. For those who have no understanding of keyboards, wordprocessors, or CVs, they can be a valuable tool.

Learning Skills

Closely allied and often combined with a word-processing facility are programs that teach job-seeking skills, for example, handling interviews, making applications and so on. Some use the process of applying for or seeking a job, to start a retrospective self-assessment and guidance process for those who haven't thought about it before now. Computer-assisted learning is another application we are familiar with from elsewhere in the education curriculum.

Multimedia

Multimedia systems are the current favourites. These may also belong to any of the other categories as well, but their unique extra quality is that they use other media such as video or audio technology in conjunction with the computer, to produce an interactive system. Examples might include; an information retrieval system, that presents video pictures of occupations, for which you have searched a computer database, or a self-assessment program that displays slides of typical activities for you to rate your own interests. There are advantages for special needs and less literate users – computers can read the words for you or show pictures. It is obvious that any software program may belong to more than one such category and that the bigger systems have sections that fit into several different categories. This too, raises larger issues that need to be dealt with separately.

The Role of Computer-assisted Guidance

There are important questions about how we use computer-assisted guidance and how it should be integrated with the rest of our work and resources. The computer is not just a tool in guidance, it is also an agent of change and using it will highlight key issues about what careers education and guidance is, who should do it, and how.

In the first place there are theoretical considerations. The use of a computer program is not a neutral act. It involves choices about values and objectives. At the most basic level, it is obvious that computer programs are written by human beings and may reflect the values and beliefs of those people. It is important to evaluate what the theoretical basis for a program is and whether this fits with our own policy and objectives. A program, that, in assessing interests, tended to confirm gender stereotypical notions of what it is appropriate to do for a living, would clearly conflict with our equal opportunities policy and practice. More subtle considerations may also be important. If the theory of guidance or occupational choice on which a program is based is different from that of the adviser who uses it to help a client, there may be an undesirable discontinuity, and the client may see the guidance given as fragmented or even contradictory. Moreover, the self-assessment inventories many computer programs now use, may simply hold up a mirror to 'nature' and reflect back the stereotypical or undeveloped awareness of the user. The famous adage 'garbage in, garbage out' gains a new layer of meaning.

A second consideration has to do with the role of computer-assisted guidance in relation to psychometric testing. Although tests are nowadays commonly available in computerised as well as paper-and-pencil format, the difference is illuminating. CAGS are learning systems: it should be possible to make as many passes through the program, as many searches of the information database, as you like. Each time, the resulting display or printout should be seen as only one of a number of possible outcomes, contingent on what has been entered. Clients should be encouraged to use CAGS in this propositional fashion to model 'what if?' questions and test the effect of presenting themselves in a variety of different ways.

Most CAGS that offer self-assessment do not do so with the sort of reliability we normally expect from psychometric testing (the questions are often too few and there are no research studies to show test-retest, or parallel form reliability or even internal consistency correlations). Nor do they usually have any validity data to demonstrate, for example, that the people who got a particular set of job suggestions actually enjoyed, or were more successful at, or stayed longer in, those jobs. This does not, however, make CAGS a poor substitute for psychometric testing. While some validity data would certainly help in the case of some programs, most CAGS were never intended to be used as predictors of future performance or satisfaction. Instead they are learning systems, intended to enable the user to explore the possibilities that could arise from presenting themselves in various ways to the world of work or learning. The fact that the user can get several different results from different passes through the program, is not a weakness but a strength. At the end of a psychometric test, a client may know some relatively hard and fast things about themselves. At the end of a CAGS program she or he knows how their response affects what is available and how this can be altered to give different results.

A Substitute for a Human Adviser?

The use of CAGS in many guidance and careers education contexts is primarily intended to supplement, rather than replace, human guidance. It has a role in preparing the client or student for working with an adviser. It also has a role as a follow-up activity to a careers education lesson or to a guidance conversation with an adviser. It can function, too, as a resource within the guidance conversation. However, there may be certain occasions, and certain clients, where use of a CAGS program meets all the current needs, without further recourse to an adviser's, tutor's or teacher's time. This is not a threat to their role. If properly used, CAGS should relieve advisers and teachers of the more basic and mundane tasks of guidance, and enable them to function at a higher level of personal expertise, doing those things that only a human being can do. But what are these things? By taking over the more basic tasks, providing information, relating it to the individual, enabling them to do some basic thinking and decision making about themselves and their interests, skills and values, the computer challenges the professionals to rethink their own role. The concomitant of using CAGS effectively, is an increased opportunity and demand for careers advisers and teachers to improve and exercise their more advanced guidance skills and knowledge.

Alongside such issues of value and principle, there are practical considerations also to be borne in mind. Arguably, the greatest value will be had from CAGS, if the user is introduced to them and supported in their use. It is also important that advice is available about which program is likely to be most relevant to a student's or client's needs. The consequences of the use of CAGS in schools, or elsewhere, are likely to be an increased and more sophisticated demand for human guidance or further resources.

Integrating Resources and Services

This raises a further requirement. Where a client wants more or different information than can be supplied by the computer, they should be able to obtain from it references to take with them to the careers library or other resource centre and vice versa. It should be easy to see the continuity between these other resources, services, prospectuses, psychometric test results, placing services and so on, and CAGS. Such integration has wider implications. As the school or guidance and career service acquires more software for various purposes, it becomes more and more important to have a menu system that gives the client and members of staff an overview of what is available, and how this relates to stages in the guidance process and different types of client need. There is also a trend for one CAGS program to be linked technically with another, so that the user can move effortlessly between them. Even without this, it is important that clients, who will increasingly use more than one program, are able to do so without necessarily requiring help.

Some larger programs are written with the idea of providing a comprehensive suite of guidance programs (sometimes termed a maxi-system), but the practical needs of day-to-day school or guidance centre work suggest a less integrated approach. This, then, necessitates extra care to ensure that integrated use is possible where it is needed. If you are looking for integration of your guidance programs, menu software now exists that allows even the average computer user to set up their own menus, covering all the guidance programs available on one computer or network. In a school context it may often be possible to involve students, whose knowledge of IT may be greater than the careers coordinator's, in the task of putting such a system together.

If your computer operates in a Windows environment, it is already possible to switch from one program to another without closing either of them. So you could move from a self-assessment program to a database, to a decision aid and back again in a matter of minutes. One practical point of all this, is that it is no longer meaningful to think of one program for use in guidance. Increasingly, we have to think in terms of the possibilities of using one program with another. We then have to think of the coherence of one program with another, for example, how far does the interest and skills assessment use categories that can be used in our databases and careers libraries. This coherence has to be self-evident to the user, the client, as well as the adviser. It is an intellectual, rather than technical, coherence.

Yet it is also linked to buying decisions. Increasingly, suppliers with some years of experience in this field, are offering packages of programs to meet a range of guidance needs and types of intervention. Buying from one supplier, rather than another, is about deciding what your next possible purchase might be, as well as the current one. It also requires the teacher, tutor or adviser, to think through larger issues about how far they want to be tied in with the total offering of this supplier, how much of the guidance and careers education process they would like to support with information technology, and whether the values, resources and processes this package may bring with it, relate comfortably with the kind of things they believe about guidance and with their general approach to education, as well as the identified needs of the clients or students they will be working with. For in the end, it is, as always, the needs of real people that must be paramount.

Computers force us to think about them, and about our principles and practice, because they make new ways of working possible. They are complex machines and the more complex a machine is, the more likely it is to change the way we do things. Not only can you do more complex things more quickly and simply and with less initial expertise, but you will be faced with choices about what to do with time saved, and how to deal with the new demands generated by the use of CAGS, as well as the issues raised about matters of value or principle. To some extent, this is true when you introduce it to any business, but when it is guidance or careers education that is involved, it is especially important to think through the implications. Careers education and guidance is very much about freedom, access, values, roles and interpersonal relationships, and the realisation of individual potential. All of these may be influenced or affected by the way we use this technology in the future.

CHAPTER 9

MEDIA EDUCATION AND CAREERS EDUCATION AND GUIDANCE
(or, I once saw a happy episode of *EastEnders*)

Ken Fox

In this chapter I will explore the possibilities for classroom discussion and activities generated from linking media education, in particular the concept of representation, with careers education and guidance. At primary and secondary school levels, media education aims to develop systematically students' critical and creative skills as producers and consumers of media products. As my sub-title suggests, the medium I will focus on is television, but I will also suggest other classroom activities using magazines, newspapers, film and photography.

Let me take you on a trip down TV's memory lane. I am a child of the sixties so TV has been part of my cultural experience from about the age of four. When I gave any thought to what I wanted to be when I grew up, it usually involved an association with one of my favourite TV characters. In my case, aged eight or nine, the favourite character was *Joe 90*, a 10-year-old boy who could take on the brain patterns of any expert (usually a rocket scientist or a secret agent) and solve problems in the adult world. I should mention that *Joe 90* was a puppet, out of the same basket as *Thunderbirds* and *Captain Scarlet*. My parents had obvious cause to be concerned: their son wanted a career as a puppet.

I use this example to illustrate the sometimes unrealistic expectations students can have about career opportunities after watching fictional representations of these careers on television, but also to highlight the possibilities to which they can be introduced through the TV portrayal of certain occupations. When Charlene (played by Kylie Minogue), a character in the Australian soap opera *Neighbours*, became a motor mechanic, the interest by young women in such a male-dominated occupation increased significantly. The students of the 1990s are steeped in media culture. Their knowledge of TV, video, music television, radio, computers, cable and satellite helps to shape their perception of the world.

The central concern of this chapter is to investigate how the world of work is represented in the media, particularly television, and to outline how students can be encouraged to become more critically aware of these representations without negating the imaginative possibilities sometimes offered by these media portrayals.

Cliffhanging from the Chalkface

With the help of Mike Walton, Head of the Social Education Department at Chaucer Technology School, Canterbury, I took a mixed-ability year 10 class through the following classroom discussion and activities. Mike observed the sessions and his commentary proved very useful in reflecting on how the students had responded. Although these activities were developed initially with Key Stage 3 students the general principle of merging some critical appraisal of media representations with the gathering of information about career choices, could be modified to cover the range of Key Stages from 2 to 4.

Classroom Discussion and Activity

The class was asked to brainstorm the names of TV programmes where the world of work is represented. After initial clarification that I was looking for examples from fictional as well as non-fictional programmes, the students supplied a long list. They were then asked to consider whether any programme they had seen recently had made them think: 'That's what I want to do when I leave school'. At first I had to work hard to get responses from them and, on reflection, this question might receive a better response after the students had gone through the other activities. Some of the students who did respond had a certain ironic tone: for example, 'I wanted to be a lifeguard after seeing *Baywatch*'. Another response by one of the dominant personalities in the class, that he wanted to be a fireman when he was young because of his affection for *Thomas the Tank Engine*, generated good humour and helped to break the ice with the rest of the class. Various forces were at work in the class dynamic. The class were testing me out as a visiting teacher, but their initial reluctance in responding to my questions about their media habits and tastes also stemmed from peer pressure.

The next activity had the students working in pairs or threes with the task of identifying, from photocopied TV schedules in the *Radio Times*, all the programmes that were concerned with or mentioned the world of work. On reflection, I probably made the task too complicated by asking the students to categorise the programmes as fiction or non-fiction. I should have discussed these categories with them before setting the task. After some clarifying remarks, the students set about their task with good humour and collaborative skill. As I walked around the room to give advice and guidance where necessary, it was noticeable that many of the students' conversations often consisted of the re-creation of scenes from their favourite programmes, where the world of work figured prominently.

The groups stayed on task and produced a variety of lists that I used as a basis for discussion. In the final activity, I asked the students to consider, from the lists they had made, which occupations dominated in the TV representations of the world of work. In my debriefing session with Mike after the lesson, he expressed his surprise at the enthusiasm of the responses from some of the students who normally remained tight-lipped in other careers and guidance discussion sessions. These opening activities supplied me with much valuable information about the students' viewing habits. The information offered by the class was detailed and insightful. I was able to decide which programme excerpt I would show them in the follow-up session.

Summary of Activities and Questions

1. Brainstorm with the students the range of programmes they view that have representations of the world of work.
2. Ask them what memories they have of TV characters or programmes that, as a child or adolescent, made them think: 'That's what I want to be when I leave school'.
3. Identify, from photocopied TV schedules in the *Radio Times*, the number and type of programme that is concerned with or mentions the world of work.
4. Produce a list of characters' names from the students' favourite programmes and ask the students to identify the type of work they do.
5. Discuss how their liking for a particular character might influence their thinking about the occupation of that character.
6. List the occupations that tend to dominate in the lives of fictional TV characters.

Return to the Chalkface: the Story So Far

The second session took place two weeks later and, after some informal banter about the TV programmes the students had viewed the previous night, I asked the class to take part in an observation activity. I explained that we would be looking at an excerpt from one of their favourite TV programmes later in the session, so this introductory task would sharpen their powers of observation. Using a photograph of a high street scene featuring a bank entrance, pedestrians, traffic (in particular a London bus), I asked the students to look carefully at the image for one minute and then, on my instructions, cover it. The students were divided in pairs or threes with their own photocopy of the image. They were then advised of the scenario whereby they were witnesses at the scene, just before a bank robbery had taken place. I took the role of the detective and posed a series of questions that focused on their visual memory and recall. The students were very adept at identifying the specific visual details, but also at extrapolating information about the period when the photograph was taken. This activity is developed from a very useful, if somewhat dated, series of images in *Eye-openers I* (Bethell, 1979) to stimulate observational skills and image analysis work.

The activity lasted approximately ten minutes and led on to the screening of the opening ten minutes of an episode of the popular soap opera *EastEnders.* Regular soap opera viewers will know that soap opera, in particular *EastEnders,* is often accused of being downbeat and pessimistic. In the episode I used with the students, Michelle's good news about her job application was sustained throughout the programme to a final scene of celebration at the Queen Vic, the local pub. In this particular episode Michelle, one of the central characters who has grown from teenager to adult in the course of the programme's first ten years, receives news that she has been successful with a job interview. One of the strengths of the serial story form used in soap opera is that story-lines can be developed over a long period of time. Michelle's frustrating search for employment happened on a weekly basis over a period of several months since she completed her college course, rather than being played out in a sensationalist one episode move from college to work. As is to be expected in soap opera, Michelle's news is but one of the story lines going on in this opening segment. The audience is taken to three other sites within the location of Albert Square, where the world of work is the dominant theme.

The series of questions I devised, to get the students thinking about these representations of work, succeeded in provoking a range of interesting comments about Michelle, work in a cafe, the difficulties of working in the service sector, and the fragmented nature of the work shown in the fictional world created in *EastEnders.* The world created in *EastEnders* is a media construction of East End life, so 'true-to-lifeness' can be a very confusing principle in analysing the way the world of work is represented in the series. However, in the urban environment that the programme reconstructs, where work is constituted by its part-time nature, permanent jobs are very rare, self-employment, shift work and unemployment reflect an image of the working world that is probably more accurate in our modern, fragmented society than the nine-to-five occupations still dominating the careers and guidance landscape. Programmes such as *EastEnders*, *Casualty* and *The Bill*, do not portray the life of *real* East Enders, *real* nurses or doctors or paramedics, or *real* policewomen, but the dramatic content can have an 'emotional realism' that touches the audience and provokes thought about such issues as the world of work, which can, in turn, play a part in students' career expectations and choices.

My regular viewing of *Please Sir*, the late 1960s early 1970s situation comedy starring a bumbling but good-hearted John Alderton, was not the stimulus for my career as a teacher. I doubt if I would be encouraged to join the teaching profession having viewed Jimmy McGovern's recent series *Hearts and Minds*. As a teacher, I can recognise the representation of my world of work as heavily dramatised and concentrated in action for the purpose of television storytelling. However, there are moments in the series when I can identify with the frustration, joy, exhaustion and motivation felt by the central character. The 'true-to-lifeness' of the series becomes less important than the 'emotional realism' it can convey. From my discussion with the students, following the excerpt from *EastEnders*, some similar identification with character and situation was evident in their remarks. Enabling students to examine media texts such as *EastEnders* in terms of its constructed nature is a possible jumping-off point for developing in more detail the conceptual links between media education and careers education and guidance.

Sequence of Activities and Questions in Session Two

1. Engage the students in an observation task with the emphasis on visual memory and recall.
2. Choose an excerpt from a programme popular with the class where the world of work is a central theme, for example, a soap opera, *Casualty*, *London's Burning*, *Soldier, Soldier, The Bill*.
3. Devise a series of questions to provoke discussion and close viewing of the excerpt: the *EastEnders* questions are general enough to be modified for a range of other programmes.
    *   How many occupations are mentioned in the excerpt?
    *   Name and describe the workplaces we are shown.
    *   What type of work do we see going on?
    *   Is there much discussion about work among the characters?
    *   What representations of the world of work can be seen in programmes such as *EastEnders*?

Follow-up questions not covered in the two sessions with the year 10 class
1. How many situation comedies use the workplace as the centre for their comedy? Are particular occupations regularly portrayed as sites for comedy?
2. How are specific parts of the job application process portrayed, if at all?
3. Do these fictional representations ever deal with issues such as harassment or bullying at work?
4. Do the representations of careers on television provide a limited range of depictions in terms of race, age or gender?
5. Do non-fiction programmes (documentaries, current affairs, advertisements etc) portray the world of work very differently from fictional programmes?

From Classroom Action to Theoretical Model

So far I have used the term representation rather unproblematically. As a key concept in media education it can be described thus: 'At its most basic, the term **representation** refers to the way images and language *actively construct* a relationship between the real world and people's ideas about it' (Swanson, 1991).

Dealing specifically with the way the world of work is actively constructed in media *representations* is outlined in Figure 9.1 (adapted from *Secondary Media Education: A Curriculum Statement*, BFI, 1991). Representation is seen as the interrelation of the *text* (in my example *EastEnders*, specifically the episode containing Michelle's good news), the *audience* (the year 10 class), and the *producers* (the BBC) and the versions of *reality* each one of these produces individually and collectively. Representation is not just concerned with the relationship between text and reality, but with judgements or choices both audiences and producers make about that relationship.

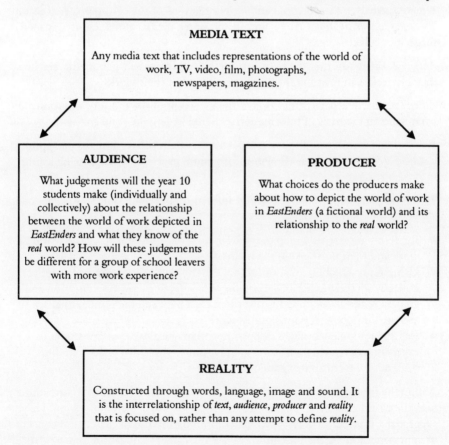

MEDIA TEXT

Any media text that includes representations of the world of work, TV, video, film, photographs, newspapers, magazines.

AUDIENCE

What judgements will the year 10 students make (individually and collectively) about the relationship between the world of work depicted in *EastEnders* and what they know of the *real* world? How will these judgements be different for a group of school leavers with more work experience?

PRODUCER

What choices do the producers make about how to depict the world of work in *EastEnders* (a fictional world) and its relationship to the *real* world?

REALITY

Constructed through words, language, image and sound. It is the interrelationship of *text, audience, producer* and *reality* that is focused on, rather than any attempt to define *reality*.

Figure 9.1 *The world of work in media representations*

A number of key issues arise from using the term representation in relation to media portrayals of the world of work.

- How can 'emotional realism' of fictional events (Michelle's good news) be considered alongside literal reality (what is it like to look for a job in the real world)?
- In what ways do media texts both limit and extend students' (audiences') frame of reference where the world of work is concerned?
- Which groups fail to be, or are inadequately represented in media portrayals of the world of work? Issues of racism, sexism and equal opportunities need to be highlighted.

How the concept of representation might inform these processes is outlined below using the specific example of researching a job in the caring professions (eg, a nurse, doctor, paramedic, etc).

Activity 1. Analyse the portrayal and representations of the caring professions on TV, eg, *Casualty*, *Cardiac Arrest*, and in the other media forms, eg, newspapers, magazines, advertising.

Activity 2. Bring together the fictional and the real image of a paramedic, see how they interrelate in forming the public perception of their work.

Activity 3. Invite a paramedic to give their perception of the job, question the paramedic on the basis of information gathered in activities one and two.

Activity 4. Set up a debate about the gaps that may exist between media perception, public perception, and on-the-job information, as a way of expressing a more informed realisation.

The concept of representation would inform the learning outcome, suggested above, in the following ways.

- Representation would help to uncover students' perceptions of the world of work and their portrayal in the media.
- Using representation as a critical tool the students are encouraged to reflect critically on the models of careers they are offered in careers education and guidance, and to see the gaps that often exist between the public, media, and on-the-job perceptions of that work.
- Representation encourages discussion and practical work about students' expectations, equal opportunities, and grounds these discussions in the student's own cultural experience.

Within the limitations of this chapter, my central concern has been to investigate how the world of work is represented in the media, particularly television. I have suggested a number of ways in which combining the use of the critical concept of representation in media education with a careers education and guidance framework, can help the students of this audio-visual age to be better informed about what they are shown of the world of work. As we enter the 21st century, our lives are likely to become even more media dominated. School leavers who are media literate may be able to take advantage of employment in the media industries, but they may also be better prepared to recognise the imaginative possibilities offered by some media portrayals of the world of work and be critical of those that offer only stereotyped representations.

While I have come to terms with the fact that a career as a *Joe 90* television puppet is not for me, I am still glad I had those dreams. As it turned out, my current job often requires that I see things from a child's point of view as a way of helping to solve problems in the adult world. Perhaps my parents still have cause to be concerned.

Professional Development and Training

This section provides a number of accounts of initiatives in professional development and training for careers teachers and careers advisers.

CHAPTER 10

PILGRIM'S PROGRESS: ENCOUNTERS IN STAFF DEVELOPMENT FOR CAREERS WORK

Bill Law

The point of careers work in schools is to help each of our young men and women to be ready to make and implement their plans for education, training, and work-life-development. This is a tall order, given that development begins in childhood and is perpetually unfolding, with education options beginning to close by the middle years of secondary education. Furthermore, in our society – continuously adjusting its social and economic structures – any kind of foresight is harder than ever to focus. Nonetheless, as each leaf of planning unfolds, we intend that each student knows what they will do, and why, that they could do something else, what the probable consequences can be, and how to deal with those consequences. Plainly, such help cannot be offered on the basis of minimal set-aside time, on the margins of timetable, leading to last-minute hit-and-run guidance. To try to do it that way is to deceive ourselves and our students.

That is why we educate our young, so that they can live and act with knowledge and understanding. Knowing and understanding work, role and self is as important as knowing and understanding anything else. And every part of the curriculum offers such insights. The arts, sciences, and technologies of our culture are our means of making such sense. What our children learn must be more than the provider of tokens, merely permitting entry to the contest. It is hardly possible for a teacher to be unaware of the work-life concerns of her or his students. It is more than ever imperative that all our teachers are offered as much help as they need in working out the professional implications of those concerns.

The Staff Development (SD) for Careers Work project examined important aspects of that help (Andrews *et al*, 1995; Law *et al*, 1995b). The project maps the SD terrain, its routes and its obstructions. It shows it to be as complex and changing as the society in which it is set. The project's findings enable us to follow a teacher (we'll call her Sarah Pilgrim) through her encounters with SD. It identifies extensive and significant options, for her and for others:

- for Sarah and other *teachers* – whether specialising or not in careers work – making use of SD provision;
- for school *management* – senior management and governors – establishing the setting in which Sarah will implement what she can learn from SD;
- for *providers* of SD – tutors, mentors and consultants – designing and delivering programmes for Sarah and others;
- for *policy makers* – in LEA, TEC, quango and Westminster – shaping the development of careers work by selectively funding and supporting parts of it.

In Initial Teacher Training

It is by no means certain that careers work would feature in initial teacher training (ITT), but for Sarah it does. Nonetheless, she finds it difficult to give it priority; her real anxieties concern how she is to manage teaching history, her main subject. History is, of course, a life skill (although in a deeper and more demanding sense than some designers of life-skill programmes care to use). Learning through other people's lives gives us each a clue to our own. But, under pressure, that point is lost on Sarah. The SD project finds: 'Where they can recall their ITT on careers work newly qualified teachers still need to work out how to apply it during their first years at school'.

The report suggests we could do more to help them:

'ITT deserves a clear rationale for the attention it pays to careers work. The rationale will suggest both how such provision is best linked to (1) the most pressing needs of new teachers and also (2) to the future development of careers work in curriculum.'

In Personal, Social and Health Education

Some may be born to careers education; some achieve it; quite a lot have it thrust upon them. Personal and Social and Health Education (PSHE) has been known to thrust it upon teachers. PSHE flows directly from a tradition of liberal education. Over many decades it has explored the boundaries of curriculum. It has developed some of the most pertinent and useful aspects of what we help our children to learn in their lives as citizens, lovers, partners, consumers – and workers. But, squeezed by all the other politically mandated pressures on the curriculum, PSHE is, too often, a frail vessel made to carry too much freight. Being asked to attend a course on 'GCSE and GNVQ options' to be covered somewhere between 'safe sex' and 'money matters' does not cause Sarah to feel good about careers education!

The problem is systemic: not so much in what teachers can or cannot do, but in the mandate, time and position they have to do it. It is an increasingly open question in which role Sarah is best able to help her students: PSHE or history. She might find in-service training for either useful; whether she can implement it is another matter.

In the System

Even the best-trained teachers cannot implement their training if they have no time, resources, mandate or acknowledgment for the work. Neither can they do it if the curriculum objectives and schemes they are expected to use turn out to be dull, sterile and out of touch with students' needs.

Sarah, a resourceful woman, can deal with much of this for much of the time; but coping with both impoverished organisational support and indifferent curriculum ideas, year-on-year, *is* wearing! The SD project has, therefore, suggested that changes in the system – in the organisation and in curriculum – must be viewed overall with changes in what teachers do. Change anywhere requires change elsewhere.

> 'Looked at from the point-of-view of how change is managed in schools, helping teachers to develop their knowledge and understanding is no more that part of the picture.
> - Staff development helps teachers do different work or do their work differently; by helping them improve their competence and understanding.
> - Programme development creates or adapts schemes of work and materials which support what teachers do, and shows how each contributes to the whole.
> - Organisation development defines the roles, provides the time, links and money and develops the policy and creates the climate which frame and succour what teachers do.'

Together the elements form a more complete – and virtuous – circle for change.

Figure 10.1 *A virtuous circle for change*

86

I am grateful to Tom Crompton of Tyneside TEC, who, during one of my rants about vicious circles for obstruction, wryly asked, 'How do we make a virtuous circle for change?'

In Careers Education and Guidance

Students can 'learn for life' in PSHE as well as in so-called 'academic' subjects. But there is also specialist careers education and guidance. Some combination of her developing interest and in being in the right place at the right time takes Sarah into specialist careers work. It gives her an interview room, a careers education resource centre and some timetable time with years 10 and 11.

Now seeking training, she finds that it is offered as short courses of half a day, or a day or so, each specifically focused on some particular tasks. The SD project found eight areas of careers work in which training might be offered: a 'careers-work repertoire'.

1. Starting points – to know how careers work is done, and why it is important.
2. Resource centre and other information work – to provide an effective information service for students and colleagues.
3. Guidance and support – to offer effective face-to-face help – in tutorial work, interviewing and counselling.
4. Reporting, recording and reviewing – to help students make best use of RoA and IAP formats and processes.
5. Careers education classroom work – to develop and deliver an effective scheme of work for careers education, in careers lessons, PSE, tutorials or subject lessons.
6. Cross-curricular work – to cooperate with other teachers in helping students to recognise and use the career relevance of their subject work.
7. Community-linked work – to establish and use effective links with parents, the business world and others in the community.
8. Managing careers work – to coordinate and organise careers work as an effective and well-established part of the organisation of the school.

Sarah learns that there is much more to careers work than doing something about 'GCSE and GNVQ options'. But the repertoire of careers work is fragmented by piecemeal training. One of the reasons for fragmentation is that different parts of the work are being supported by disconnected government funding and policy regimes; sometimes operating with different programme titles. Yet all parts of the process depend on each other for their effectiveness.

Sarah, by persistence, can get a comprehensive view of careers work. Developing a coherent view is more of a problem. Comprehensive means 'covering everything'; coherent means 'linking into a useable and effective whole'. The SD project report notes the issue: 'Some courses are better than others at offering an opportunity to understand how the various elements of careers work can be coherently integrated into an effective whole'.

In Theory as well as Practice

As courses focus on one or other aspect of an increasingly fragmented taxonomy, they also become more skill focused; in some cases explicitly addressing 'competence' as the end-point of training. The SD project suggests: 'User-driven SD provisions is more likely to be task-specific and less likely to involve theoretical elements'.

Nobody wants Sarah to be able merely to *talk* about careers-work skills that she cannot actually *deliver*. In an increasingly accountable world, skill-training helps Sarah to demonstrate 'value for money' spent on the training. But course providers do not see themselves wholly and exclusively in the skills game. The SD project report indicates the extent of their interest in theory as well as practice. The report outlines the justification. Theory:

- underpins action with an understanding of causes and effects;
- suggests new action for new – and as yet untried – circumstances;
- develops frameworks within which the diverse and evolving elements of careers-work action can be related to each other and to a whole.

Sarah is persuaded in her training that there is nowt so practical as good theory. Good theory helps her to anticipate the consequences of her actions and understand why they happen in that way. It provides her with rational bases for new action. She needs to be able to suggest different action for different students, in different settings, and at different stages of development. As a careers specialist she increasingly sees herself not just as a *replicating* technician but as a *reflective* professional. Furthermore, and in an increasingly politicised service, she needs to know and understand how helpful, or otherwise, policy imperatives are likely to be. She can't do everything that everybody thinks she should do; she needs to know and understand what is worth doing.

In Careers Coordination

A resourceful teacher, with a sceptical intelligence, can do much for careers education. Such qualities have won Sarah the position of careers coordinator. She knows that no school can uniformly sustain everything in the careers-work repertoire. She works with colleagues to identify what can and should be done. She has come full circle, looking again at how history, with other subjects, can inform and enable students in their approach to adult and working life.

Sarah needs, therefore, to attract the interested attention of her colleagues. That means getting to know them and their preoccupations. She cannot afford to be another problem; her credibility depends on being part of the solution. And so she becomes a *provider* of SD. But training courses, even held 'on-site', are not the only way – certainly not the best – of canvassing colleagues' preoccupations and negotiating with their intentions. There are, however, options. The SD project identifies a range (the project lists them in detail, with support and planning material, in Law *et al*, 1995b):

1. Longer courses – offering course contact time of at least five days.
2. Short courses – offering course contact time of less than five days, perhaps as little as 2–3 hours.
3. Experience-based learning – a visit to or placement in a location outside school – possibly as a work-experience placement.
4. Open learning – published packs, study guides, booklets for teachers to use in their own way.
5. Support networks – meetings to exchange ideas and information with other people.
6. Consultancy – experts working with teachers to develop aspects of your work.
7. School-based work – help provided specifically for the school's staff (some or all) including help given by colleagues.

Each type of provision brings colleagues into different patterns of contact with people, locations and learning material. The people include tutors, mentors, peers and consultants. The locations include conference centre, business premises and the school itself. The materials include physical resources and open learning material. The variety of learning scenarios created from that diversity include not only lectures, seminars, role plays and simulations, but also workshops, development work, feedback from hands-on experience and distance learning. Some of this provision can refresh aspects of change that others cannot reach (Figure 10.2)

No map can be definitive for all situations in all schools. Nonetheless, the project reports some general findings.

> 'Forms of provision which can be used close to the school can take more account of, and directly influence, programme organisation development. Consultancy, school-based work and open-learning are all capable of use in close conjunction with a particular school.'

In Open Learning

Realising this, Sarah asks her colleagues to work with one or other of the open-learning packs now available (Justice, 1991; Law *et al*, 1991a, revised 1995a; Law *et al*, 1991b; NCET, 1992; Law, 1993; NCET, 1995; Barnes, 1993). She finds that they have their own, wonderfully disrespectful, way with the material. They use some, adapt some, and discard some. Nothing is assumed, everything is challenged. They work in groups, kick ideas around, drawing on bits and pieces of the pack, dismembering it to support specific work by different teams. With Sarah and other management people on board, they are engaged in programme and organisation development, as much as staff development. Furthermore, they are using the pack in conjunction with other provision: comparing experience in their networks, linking to school-based workshops, talking with a consultant from the Careers Service.

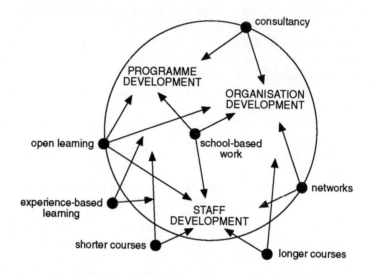

Figure 10.2 *Supporting the virtuous circle for change*

Linking a pre-programmed open-learning text with this dynamic and less tidy reality, is a problem (Wyatt, 1993). For Sarah, arriving at a recognisable programme, with a clear beginning and a visible path forward, is not easy. The SD project found likewise. 'Participants are reported to have difficulty where learning resources are diversified – particularly with regard to managing time, using the learning methods and preparing for assessment.'

Sarah must think about how to assemble such diversity into some coherence for her colleagues. Some providers are publishing support material to help with these tasks (KCGS, 1994; Law *et al*, 1995a). Assessment is an issue here. An advantage of open learning is its ability to link learning to experience: in the place, on the tasks and among the people directly involved. Sarah needs an open-assessment arrangement that matches the openness of the learning scenario.

The SD project reports: 'There is a movement towards portfolio development as the procedure verifying a basis for accreditation'.

There are schemes to which she could link her programme, and which can provide such accreditation opportunities (listed in Law *et al*, 1995b).

In Conclusion

Staff development for careers work offers a dynamic and complex series of transactions; relating to the needs of young women and men for whom 'what next?' is a daunting challenge as well as beckoning hope; engaging the attention of teachers in all kinds of positions; influenced by the action of all kinds of stakeholders. In such a situation, a simple-minded approach to 'training' is not inevitably nor exclusively 'the solution'. Change, in a noisy and besieged system like a school, is more demanding of our inventiveness than that. And, if training and other SD provision does manage to change what a woman like Sarah can do, then we had all better be ready for more change!

In a summary of its recommendations, the SD project suggests how, by identifying who can do something about what.

Table 10.1

	Teachers	Managers	Providers	Policymakers
Quality can be maintained and developed where provision…				
…focuses both on what teachers do to help their students and also on how the roles and tasks can be coordinated into a coherent programme	★	★	★	
…improves both competence and understanding in careers work	★	★	★	
…helps participants to select and use appropriate elements of staff development and assemble them into a coherent programme of action	★	★	★	
….helps teachers to understand how careers work, society and the economy are changing	★	★	★	
….is linked to an overall strategy for managing change in schools and college	★	★	★	
National impact will be achieved if…				
…all teachers involved in careers work have access to a support network within their locality	★	★	★	
…careers work is included in a structured induction programme for all newly qualified teachers in secondary sector, in their first year of teaching		★		

	Teachers	Managers	Providers	Policymakers
…every secondary school has at least one teacher with a professional qualification in careers work, to a minimum level of certificate in further professional studies, and has laid plans for another teacher to gain similar qualifications		★		
…all school staff-development plans include relevant SD opportunities for subject teachers and tutors contributing to careers work, as well as for the careers coordinator		★		
…all ITT programmes include an introduction to careers work in schools.			★	★
The *policy frame* to support these developments requires that…				
…there is a clear rationale for the inclusion of careers work in ITT			★	★
…support is maintained for courses which can maintain a supply of well-qualified teachers for this work			★	★
…funding arrangements, such as are provided by the GEST category for careers education and guidance, and the years 9–10 initiative, are maintained at appropriate levels				★
…positive support for careers work, setting out expectations for quality as well as quantity in delivery, is made explicit in policy-related statements				★
…the terms in which OFSTED inspections attend to careers work cover all its aspects, and identify the needs for further staff development.				★

Staff development for careers work offers more options for the improvement of our children's education than we have yet fully realised. But responsibility for its achievement cannot be off-loaded on to teachers: it depends upon the willing and comprehending operation of all stakeholders.

CHAPTER 11

REFLECTIVE ACTION PLANNING: A MODEL FOR CONTINUING PROFESSIONAL DEVELOPMENT

David Frost

In launching the recent Teacher Training Agency (TTA) strategy documents Mrs Gillian Shephard was quoted as saying 'we can't afford to spend GEST funds on in-service training which does not lead directly to school improvement' (*Times Educational Supplement*, 31 March 1995). The initiative currently being undertaken by the TTA began with a statement which emphasised the *focus* of GEST (Grant for Education Support and Training) spending and the possibility of targeting funds on particular priority areas, but again no mention is made of the variety of approaches to the delivery of staff development or in-service training (INSET). What I believe the TTA should be interested in is the matter of the nature and quality of provision rather than what that provision is focused upon.

The Problem of Delivery

The problem has always been with the notion of *courses*. Whether they take place in the school, in a hotel or in a university seminar room, the effect can be the same. They often empower those who are delivering rather than the course members. Of course, the course leaders will often want to support or encourage some kind of professional action or another, but school staff development coordinators still report that they find it difficult to ensure that their school reaps the benefit in return for the money spent on sending individual members of staff on such INSET programmes. What has often been missing is a means by which individual teachers can be empowered to develop and improve both their own professional practice and the practices of the institution or organisation.

As an HEI tutor committed to professional development and school improvement, I have worked with colleagues in schools and in a number of Careers

Services to develop an approach to INSET which I believe has the potential to support not only the professional learning of individuals but also lead in a direct and immediate way to school or organisational improvement. I have referred to this as 'reflective action planning'.

Reflective Action Planning

The essential principle underpinning this approach is the commitment to making a direct link between the individual's professional learning and the development priorities of the institution or organisation. It is most likely to be successful when supported by an award-bearing scheme, although there is no reason why the model could not be used without the benefit of accreditation. The model is represented in Figure 11.1 and I shall proceed to discuss each of the component parts.

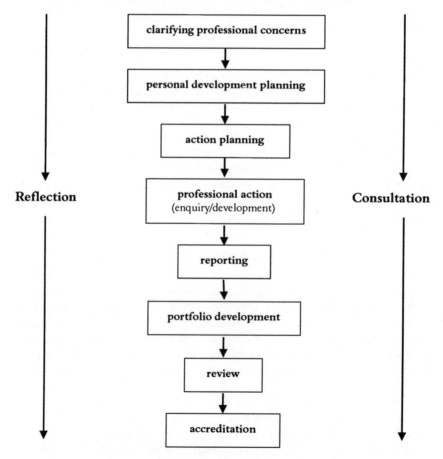

Figure 11.1 *The reflective action planning model*

This model is not one of staff development – a term which implies something which is planned and delivered by senior management or outside agencies employed by senior management – rather, it is a model of professional development which starts from the assumption that the point of the exercise is to support the individual professional practitioner who wants to take responsibility for their own professional learning.

1. Clarifying the Professional Concerns

If I want to adopt a more systematic approach to my own professional development I need first to clarify what my professional concerns are and this entails becoming clear about my professional role and responsibilities. This is not as straightforward as it might sound and it is surprisingly effective to sit down and deliberately think this through. Colleagues report that opportunities for this kind of reflection are rare and precious and, although a good appraisal scheme will facilitate this, it is likely to be on a two-year cycle which is not sufficiently regular or continuous.

The act of writing down a statement for myself about my role and responsibilities, enables me to think about my experience, expertise and future career development. The written statement serves a number of purposes: first it is of itself reflective and can lead to fresh insights; secondly, it results in a document which can be discussed with others if this is appropriate, and thirdly, it serves as an introductory item in a professional development portfolio.

2. The Personal Development Plan

Development planning in schools is now well established, but how many teachers can say that they have played a full part in the development of that corporate plan? The DES guidelines issued in 1989 have been widely interpreted as support for a 'top-down' approach, which does not encourage practitioners to develop a sense of ownership and commitment to the agreed goals of the school or organisation.

The reflective action planning process on the other hand fosters what we might call 'bottom-up development planning'. With the support of an external facilitator such as an HEI tutor, I am able to summarise my role and responsibilities and set out the implications in terms of the focus of my development work over the forthcoming 12-month period. I can sort out my priorities for both curriculum and organisational development and, together with the implications for my own professional learning, set them out clearly in writing, as in the example overleaf.

PERSONAL DEVELOPMENT PLAN
Edmundo Ross

Roles and responsibilities

I am a science teacher in the third year of my teaching career. I have been contributing to the review and re-writing of schemes of work and see myself continuing to do so throughout the coming academic year. However, I am also a group tutor in year 10 and I am interested in developing the pastoral side of my work.

Focus for development

I recently read a report in the TES about student councils – elected student bodies -- which give students a direct involvement in decision making in the school. I followed this up by attending a conference about citizenship and am now very keen to pursue this idea. It seems to present real opportunities for children to learn citizenship and to enable us to develop a greater sense of the school as an inclusive community. I would like to explore the possible development of a student council in the school.

I realise that such a development would demand management skills which I may not have and so would want to talk with RS (deputy head) about strategies for managing the consultation process and the implementation of such a project.

Development priorities

I realise that the student council project, if it is approved, will be very time consuming especially in the developmental stage. The process of consultation would probably take the whole of the autumn term and would have to include presentations to the SMT, the whole staff and the governing body. Once the consultation process is complete, I will be able to devote more time to reviewing science modules and would imagine being able to start the review of the year 7 schemes by March next year.

Clearly it would not be appropriate to proceed to take action on the basis of such a plan without consulting with relevant colleagues. As a classroom teacher, I need to consult with senior managers and others who may have a broader view of the development priorities of the school as a whole. What I perceive to be my priorities may well match closely the priorities set out in the school development plan. On the other hand it may be that I have to adjust my priorities in the light of what my colleagues may tell me about competing priorities or constraints such as the lack of funding. If my plan is effective and well thought out, I may be able to persuade my colleagues that the school's development plan has to be adjusted to accommodate my view of developmental priorities. The important thing is that I want to be sure that I have the support of my senior managers and that we have reached an understanding about goals that are realistic.

3. Action Planning

If I am going to be able to pursue my development priorities effectively, I need to think through the action steps systematically. I also need to consult with colleagues about such steps; there may be implications for support from colleagues or for resources and, if I am to achieve what I set out to achieve, I need to set realistic targets with dates for reporting and reviewing progress. The example below shows how I can translate one of my development priorities into a written action plan which allows me to consult with appropriate colleagues.

ACTION PLAN

Nellie Dean   **October 1994**

Focus for development
As indicated in my development plan, it is an urgent priority to develop a resource centre for careers in my school. At the moment there is a section of the library which is used for this purpose, but it is inadequate and often inaccessible. The careers resource centre was identified as a priority in the school development plan last summer and I have had an indication from Reg Maudling (Deputy Head) that we could afford to finance a new centre in two stages either side of next April.

Previous learning
I have been through this innovation before in my last school and am aware of the issues. I am reasonably confident about the practical steps I need to take. I think that I am familiar enough with the range of materials available and will not need to tackle the workbook exercise (careers work open learning programme) which deals with that.

Role development
The development of the centre will demand a degree of assertiveness and management skill because I need to negotiate a change of practice with my colleagues. I also need to secure an increased resource allocation. I shall look at the 'Managing careers work' section to see if there are exercises or ideas there to help me.

Curriculum development
I shall use the 'Priorities for development' exercise in the section about materials, just to check that I have dealt with the matter of materials adequately. I shall then use the 'Who uses your centre?' exercise to develop my understanding abut patterns of use and the possible links with the curriculum.

Organisational development
I need to rethink the role of the centre and its place in the school as a whole. I also need to enable the senior management team to do the same. The 'Priorities for development' exercise in the 'Ideal resource centre' section should be helpful here.

Reporting
I shall submit my proposals to the senior management team by 31 January in the form of a two sided report with costings attached.

Evidence for the portfolio
- copy of a leaflet about the resource centre in my previous school
- copies of audit materials in the resource centre at my previous school
- photocopies of the task sheets from workbook exercises named above
- a summing up of the findings from my conversations with form tutors
- my paper setting out proposals for the new centre.

Review and target setting
I have arranged with my line manager (she is also my mentor) to review my action plan and discuss my embryonic proposals on the second day of next term. I shall then firm them up by the end of the month.

This particular action plan was written by an individual who happened to be participating in an advanced certificate in careers education and guidance course using the Open College programme, but the format would be useful in any context. The last section clearly arises from the need to submit evidence for accreditation, but I would suggest that portfolio development would be useful without the accreditation arrangement.

4. Professional Action (enquiry/development)

The sample action plan above includes professional development, curriculum development and organisational development which need to be integrated if worthwhile improvements are to take place. In each case we see the use of common sense methods of enquiry of the sort that practitioners can easily build into their routine development work.

Let me illustrate further by taking an example of a professional concern and considering the approach to enquiry and development. If I am a careers teacher wanting to develop careers education modules in year 10, I am bound to have a number of questions such as the following.

- How can they be dovetailed with other PSE dimensions?
- What are the most important needs of year 10 students?
- What alternative schemes of work could we use?

Conducting professional enquiry to support this development will have to be shaped by the amount of time I have and the politics of the situation, so I might consider asking someone in the Careers Service to identify examples of good practice in other schools in the area so that I could contact my 'opposite number' and ask how they do it there. I might consider asking the PSE team if I could put a number of alternative approaches to the next team meeting – perhaps a short paper describing them might be most efficient. I could record my colleagues' responses and agree to come back with a revised proposal in the light of the points made at the meeting. I might also consider reading some theoretical account of the needs of 14/15-year-olds and then testing this out by seeking the views of the students. How best to do this though? Do I really need to ask all of the year 10 students what they think? Could I really get a helpful picture of their experiences and perceptions through a questionnaire administered to over a hundred young people? How detailed and insightful will their responses be? How much time will it take me to analyse the completed questionnaires? Surely my understanding of the issues will be better served by having a really good conversation with a couple of small groups of students. Such common-sense enquiry strategies can easily be documented and justified within a portfolio of evidence. The point is that if it makes professional sense it should be credit worthy in academic terms provided the HEIs can adapt their practice to include the presentations of portfolios.

5. Reporting

One of the difficulties with the kind of INSET which involved the individual taking time off from their day to day work in order to attend a short course, is the lack of effective feedback for the school or organisation. When I am planning to take action to address an agreed development priority, I recognise that I am accountable to my colleagues and that I have an obligation to report the outcomes to appropriate audiences within the school or organisation. In this case reporting is not merely some kind of 'tokenistic' feedback, but an essential and integral part of the professional documentation arising from ongoing consultation with managers and colleagues in the school or organisation.

If I were to set myself the task of evaluating the students' use of the Careers Resource Centre for example, it would be unthinkable for me to neglect to produce a written report for the SMT – such a report would include my findings and recommendations. If this were to be done verbally or on the back of the proverbial envelope, it would not carry weight. I have to consider the possible audiences – senior managers, OFSTED, the governors perhaps – and their need to know.

6. Portfolio Development

The documentary evidence arising from the systematic pursuit of development priorities can be assembled in the form of a portfolio. The word 'portfolio' suggests a collection of separate items rather than a single document, but it is a collection which is organised and assembled with the aid of devices to make it coherent. The portfolio has a number of possible purposes. It is a clear and accessible body of evidence – evidence of what I have achieved and of my current plans – which enables me to:

- maintain a clear sense of momentum and direction;
- reflect on the issues;
- consult and get support from my mentor, appraiser, manager, colleague or critical friend;
- present a summative record of achievement for the purposes of appraisal or career development;
- make a submission for the purposes of accreditation.

It would be wrong to imagine that the assembling of a portfolio is in some way easier than writing a more traditional academic paper. Portfolio development itself demands skills of organisation and presentation. It is vital that all items in a portfolio are clearly identified according to audience and purpose. The structure of the portfolio and the style of presentation should be determined by the individual writer, but portfolios will have to include different kinds of commentary according to the different levels of accreditation being sought.

7. Review

The process of innovation, improvement and development rarely unfolds in the way it was planned as Michael Fullan has reminded us, 'change is a journey not a blueprint' (Fullan, 1993). So I need to stop and, with my colleagues, take stock of where we have got to and evaluate the change. Whatever targets and goals we agreed at the outset may have become redundant or at least need a rethink. The process of bottom-up development planning depends on individuals being prepared and able to sit down with colleagues and review, so that the school's development plan remains an organic working plan and not an inert document handed down from above.

8. Accreditation

The process of accreditation is based on the fundamental principle that credit should be given for professional learning arising in the workplace or related closely to professional tasks. Accreditation should provide not only recognition and career development through the award of higher professional qualifications, but it should also provide support and guidance from HEI tutors. The tutor's role should be to:

- provide a forum for discussion of curricular issues;
- provide the individual with guidance on enquiry strategies and reading;
- provide guidance on the production of evidence;
- challenge the individual's assumptions and developing theories;
- support the reflective action planning process.

The submission of a portfolio is a satisfying experience, which is very motivating for the individual concerned and a considerable source of pride. An extract from a teacher's portfolio illustrates some of the benefits of this approach.

EXTRACT FROM A PORTFOLIO

As evidence of my professional development this portfolio functions on two levels, one explicit, the other implicit. On the explicit level there is evidence of my achievements in terms of curriculum development and of improvement in my professional skills. For example, it shows that I have developed and implemented new science modules and that I have developed the ability to plan more systematically; it also indicates that I have become a teacher-researcher. On the implicit level: when I look back over the way I have used language in the introduction, in the critical narrative and in the detailed evidence of curriculum development, I am aware of a profound change in my approach and in the level of my professional maturity.

During the writing of this portfolio and in the generation of the work that it documents, I have become very interested in broader, less subject specific issues of education, in particular the notion of student democracy and young people's rights within the education system. I have found ideas which are important and powerful, expressed in unlikely places, for example, the matter of 'a sense of awe and wonder' referred to in the OFSTED documentation. My level of professional confidence has increased greatly and the benefits to my teaching and learning of the students in my classes are immeasurable and ever-increasing. The power of critical, supported self-review is incredible and it provides a sense of pace and a change to my teaching.

I have recently become involved in plans for the new sixth form at my school and the world of GNVQ learning has opened up to me. The issues this programme raises about the Key Stage 3 and 4 curriculum, in terms of relevance and learning style, have echoes in the nature of my own reflective action planning work over the past two years.

Self-evaluation and independent initiative-based activities are the foundations of GNVQ and these are areas which interest me in terms of my future development. I feel that I am now a professional, far more at ease with myself, although still aware and alert for difficulties, short-comings and what I have yet to get right about my own practice. In my mind there exists this perfect ideal of what a teacher should be, a platonic purity, and then there is me – the actuality. By working with this structure for analysis and development, I find that I can systematically make adaptations to my teaching and continue to develop my understanding. It is an empowering and invigorating process. I am a learner free to explore and develop in a learning environment.

Andrew Wright, Angley School

As Figure 11.1 indicated, there are two parallel and continuous processes: reflection and consultation. These processes are to some extent interrelated, but it is nonetheless important to maintain a boundary between them. Reflection is potentially private and can deal with matters which are sensitive and highly political, whereas consultation is necessarily public, and quite properly the business of the school as an organisation.

Reflection

Reflection is an integral part of the exercise of professional judgement. We would not be able to function in terms of the minute-by-minute decision making without what Schon (1983) called 'reflection in action'. More deliberate reflection is essential in order to make sense of the complexity of professional action and to develop fresh perspectives on professional issues.

Reflection also enables me to experience a sense of achievement by heightening my awareness about my action and about the extent of my professional learning. The process needs therefore to include reflection which is built in to the change process, and reflection which is summative. Let me illustrate by looking at some of the key opportunities for reflection. When I begin the process of reflective action planning I need first to reflect on my current professional predicament. I need to clarify for myself:

- my role in the organisation;
- my professional responsibilities;
- my experience and current capability in relation to this role and these responsibilities.

This is best done as an initial statement which introduces a portfolio. It is essentially a private matter which would not necessarily be shown to a senior colleague although it might be helpful to discuss my development priorities with them.

The process of reflection should be continuous and those receiving external tutorial support are encouraged to keep a journal and to discuss their entries with the tutor. A journal enables me to record and retrieve at a later date not only the curriculum or management issues but my feelings and thoughts about my own professional and personal development. My journal, together with all the evidence accumulated in the portfolio enables me to write a summative reflection which serves a number of purposes. First, it helps me to make sense of my experience and to crystallise the professional learning which has taken place; secondly, I am able to become clearer about what has been achieved and what targets I need to set myself for the future and, thirdly, I am able to ensure that I meet the particular assessment criteria when I submit the completed portfolio for accreditation.

Consultation

Central to this model of professional development is the notion that there should be a very direct link between the individual's professional learning and the development priorities of the school or organisation. Some may assume that this means that individuals will be constrained and that priorities will be set by senior managers in a top-down sort of way; it might also be assumed that the reflective action planning approach will necessarily squeeze out the type of professional development that is individual focused rather than school focused. On the contrary, I hope that what I have said about the role of reflection and personal development planning makes clear that the model is individual centred but that it should recognise that individuals work in organisations and, to that extent, their professional development can only make sense in relation to the goals of that organisation. This means that there are crucial elements of the reflective action-planning process which demand that the individual consults with appropriate colleagues. The development plan includes a statement about the individual's development priorities so there has to be some discussion and agreement about those priorities to ensure that they correspond with the school's corporate development plan. This consultation provides an opportunity for the individual to have some direct influence over the school's development plan. Similarly, action plans need to be the subject of consultations because they will lead to substantial change in practice or to the carrying out of enquiry/development work which is likely to affect a wide range of colleagues and students.

School- or Area-based Support

The reflective action-planning process is likely to be effective, if it is supported both by the individual's school/organisation and by an external agency with appropriate skills and materials: a partnership approach. I shall briefly look at the roles of the institution and of the external agency.

1. Support from the institution – the management of the school or organisation need to ensure that:
    - adequate external support is brought in and provided, with space and suitable timeslots in which to operate;
    - individuals have clear reference points for consultation (whether in the form of a mentor, team leader, line manager, critical friend, appraiser etc);
    - the process of corporate development planning is sufficiently open and flexible to allow for 'bottom-up' participation;
    - there is good liaison with the external support agency.
2. Support from the external agency – the external agents need to provide:
    - effective guidance to support a reflective action-planning process;
    - a programme of seminars and workshops to deliver both support for the process and input on relevant subject matter;
    - individual tutorial support appropriate to the level of accreditation sought;
    - access to literature.

Since the whole purpose of this approach is to support professional development which will lead directly to school improvement, it is fairly obvious that the support should be arranged in a location which will cause less disruption to the participants. Ideally the support should be school-based with group sessions taking place in 'twilight' slots although this is not without its difficulty: busy professionals are often tired by this time and steps need to be taken to lift the mood and energy levels. If the scale of the operation is not sufficiently large to warrant siting in a single school, then an area-based or consortium approach should be considered. Drawing as it would from a number of different schools, this also has the advantage of creating opportunities for networking and for the sharing of ideas and comparisons of practice.

Adapting the Model

The reflective action-planning model can easily be adapted and used to support different kinds of in-service projects. For example, if a school wants to provide a management training course for middle managers which might include a series of workshops on such matters as 'team building' and 'budgeting and resource management', the participants can be asked to conduct a self-assessment exercise, to set targets for development and to pursue those learning targets through a series of action plans. The resulting portfolio could lead to a management related award. In contrast, a group of teachers may wish to set up a curriculum development support group which could be enhanced by the process of reflective action planning leading to a master's level qualification in curriculum development. Clearly, the guidance material which supports the participants would have to be modified to suit the particular context, and to describe the assessment criteria relevant to the award for which the individual has registered. This model has been used in open learning contexts and in relation to school working parties convened to address particular priorities such as those identified through an OFSTED inspection.

Conclusion

Some years ago Professor Jean Rudduck said:

> 'If we are interested in substantial curriculum change, we may need to find structures and resources to help teachers to re-examine their purposes... and feel more in control of their professional purposes and direction. Some sense of ownership of the agenda for personal action is, in my view, a good basis for professional development and professional learning.' (Rudduck 1988, p.210)

I hope that I have described here a model of professional development which has the potential to put practitioners in the driving seat as far as their own professional learning is concerned. I hope also that I have demonstrated how that professional development process can both be shaped by and can contribute to the institutional development planning process in a way which leads directly and effectively to school improvement. This 'bottom-up development planning' approach is designed to enable practitioners to reclaim their professionalism and to experience a genuine sense of ownership over educational change.

CHAPTER 12

THE CAREERS WORK TRAINING PARTNERSHIP

Helen Reynolds and David Frost

This chapter provides an account of a successful partnership between a higher education institution and local authority officers (whether from the Careers Service or the Advisory Service), established to support and accredit professional, curricular and organisational development for careers teachers and advisers using the open learning programme, 'Careers Work'.

Background

The network began in 1991 with a collaboration between Kent Careers and Guidance Service and Canterbury Christ Church College and, at the time of writing, extends over 14 local authority areas. The form of accreditation provided by the college rests on the reflective action-planning model (see Chapter 11 for a detailed account), which enables the participants to build up a portfolio of evidence of both the learning activities arising from their use of the open learning materials and from the school-based development work related to the programme. This particular combination of open learning and portfolio-based accreditation was seen to be valuable because it has the potential to support improvement of practice and institutional change by supporting participants' systematic enquiry and curriculum development. The open learning materials provided the main 'content' of the course, while the action-planning approach provided the 'process'.

The Nature of the Support

A fundamental principle established at the outset was that most of the support should be provided in locations close to participants' work places. The course would not make demands on participants in terms of time out of school or time-consuming attendance at the college. Members of the career service support team were inducted as associate tutors of the college so that they could deliver support locally.

At the end of the first year, a number of other Careers Services and local authority teams joined the partnership so that the programme could be offered in East Sussex, Surrey and Staffordshire. The team of associate tutors expanded accordingly and so the original team set out to produce a tutors' guide which would have a general application for those wishing to support an open learning based professional development programme. The lessons learnt from our early experiences were all incorporated into the guide (KCGS, 1994) which was published with the help of funding from Kent Training and Enterprise Council. The guide for tutors set out vital steps in the process of setting up a framework of support for careers teachers and advisers who wish to use a Careers Work open learning programme.

1. A first step is to form a network of associate tutors and to provide opportunities to share ideas about strategies for running group sessions and for providing individual support. The nature of evidence for the portfolio is also a key theme for discussion.

2. The group of tutors need to organise their recruitment and selection procedures so that the most appropriate participants are identified. We have discovered that it is vital to recruit only those who really want to use an open learning approach to their professional development.

3. Potential participants need to be provided with pre-course guidance materials which enable them to explore their learning styles and to establish the conditions which will support them throughout the course; for example, a school-based mentor needs to be identified and the senior management team need to be consulted about the impact the programme is likely to have on the institution.

4. Participants need to be invited to a preparatory workshop which enables them to explore in detail the nature of the course before making a firm commitment.

5. Tutors need to plan a joint orientation and induction conference to kick start the programme. As our network has developed it has become necessary to stage a number of similar orientation conferences at various locations but the tutors within the network are able to collaborate to ensure a certain commonality of experience.

6. Tutors need to agree on ways in which the ongoing, local support can be delivered and this means being clear about the kind of support that participants need for portfolio development.

7. The assessment and moderation arrangements have to be put in place; it is vital to ensure common standards across the network.

8. Lastly, the tutors need to have a clear system for monitoring and evaluating the programme so that it can be continuously improved.

Working with an expanded team of tutors across a wider geographical area presented new challenges which were only partially addressed by the publication of the tutors' guide.

The Tutor Network

Ultimately, we believe that this collaboration has worked well because of the shared values of the tutors involved. The network brought together the strengths and expertise of a range of people with substantial experience in such areas as guidance practice, curriculum leadership and staff development. The particular mode of learning supported through the partnership is one which such experienced careers practitioners naturally embraced. For example, the helping skills that experienced guidance practitioners have developed are the sort that tutors need when supporting open learning and professional development based on reflective action planning. Similarly, experienced careers professionals are used to working with 'the real world'; in other words with concrete cultural experiences and high levels of relevance, and this resonates well with the way the course is focused on the improvement of professional practice. The principles underpinning records of achievement and action planning have always been accepted as core principles by careers professionals and it is these same principles which are central to this particular model of professional learning. The participant's portfolio recognises and celebrates achievement and supports the individual in setting targets and action planning to address those targets.

It is these shared values that enable the tutors who belong to the Careers Work Training Partnership to work cooperatively even across a wide geographical area. Although there are clear guidelines and express criteria for the course, we need to be clear that such a collaborative enterprise does not rely on tight specifications but rather on shared values, agreed principles and a willingness to engage in cooperative exploration and local experimentation. The regular contact and rich dialogue facilitated through this network is what really provides the coherence to this increasingly nation-wide programme.

It is important for the participants to experience a coherent programme based on a reliable partnership. They usually know the tutors from their own area already and this gives them added confidence in the course structure, but there has always been the risk that the college could appear simply a remote, demanding, administrative body with no interest in or links with the students. The participants need to know and be reminded that this is a collaborative enterprise in which all the partners play an active role.

Impact of the Programme

The network of associate tutors is maintained by regular meetings of the steering committee, which effectively manages the programme as a whole. This group meets several times a year and provides an effective forum for the exploration of practice, for moderating standards and resolving any difficulties that emerge.

The schools benefit from the course because the participants become more influential and are able to raise CEG to a position of prominence within the school. The evaluation of the programme has enabled us to improve this provision and to understand more about the impact on students' experience, although we believe that this is better revealed through the case studies in the following two chapters.

It is interesting to note that, on completing the course, a number of teachers have achieved promotion in recognition of their commitment and ability to take further responsibility.

The participants themselves have generally felt the course to be successful. The process of accreditation gives a spur to the enquiry and development process and presents students with the opportunity to evaluate the provision of careers education and guidance in their schools and develop fresh strategies for delivering it. One point in particular, frequently cited by students, is that the course leads to enormous gains in confidence, both in themselves as professionals and in the way in which careers education and guidance is perceived and valued by colleagues and students. The content of the course provides them with an easily articulated rationale for careers education and guidance, and the process of accreditation ensures that they can reflect on their own professional action and work more dynamically to bring about change in their own institution.

Conclusion

While we have a great deal of evidence to suggest that the programme is successful the Careers Work Training Partnership has a full agenda of issues to be addressed in the future. For example, we are planning a more structured induction and support programme for local support tutors and for school-based mentors.

In conclusion, we would suggest that the most significant outcome from this enterprise is that we have demonstrated that it is possible for higher education institutions, Careers Services, and schools to create a mutually supportive network of professionals committed to the qualitative improvement of careers education and guidance. If this three-way partnership continues to be genuinely collaborative and based on shared values we believe that it will be creative, transformative and empowering for all concerned.

CHAPTER 13

SUPPORTING CAREERS ADVISERS

Jackie Hartley and Mike Shaw

In September 1993, Staffordshire Careers Service decided to join the Careers Work Training Partnership (see Chapter 12) in order to support the development of careers education and guidance activities within schools. The approach seemed particularly suited to our needs because it requires participants to plan development work systematically in aspects of careers education and guidance, carry it out, gather evidence and reflect on the outcomes of the process, both in terms of their own learning and in evaluating the impact of their development work on the school. We felt that such an approach would enable practitioners to develop new skills and experience, as well as knowledge and understanding which is rooted in the workplace.

The careers advisers we enrolled had various reasons for undertaking the course. Some wanted accreditation and recognition for the work they were already doing, others wanted to refresh their knowledge of theory and boost their confidence in developing careers work in school; others wanted to use it as a means to improve contacts with other staff in the schools in which they worked.

At the outset the careers advisers expressed concern that the Open College programme was not really designed for their role in schools. In order to collect evidence for their portfolio, the programme required them to involve themselves in a whole range of school activities. Having easy access to classrooms and other curricular activities was not going to be straightforward, nor finding the extra time to engage in research and consultation. For example, Anne felt that, because she did not actually work full-time in schools, she could be disadvantaged still further:

'Because I can only spend a limited amount of time in each school
(approximately one and a half days a week in each) it makes it difficult to know
exactly what is happening and how things are changing.'

There were also issues to do with role, status and available lines of communication. Colette commented that:

'As a careers adviser, it makes it difficult to develop my own ideas as I can only make suggestions for the development of careers, to the careers team and senior management in that school, in the hope that they may want to implement them.'

Initially, some of the schools were sceptical about why careers advisers were doing this work, ostensibly intruding into areas that shouldn't concern them. Informal meetings were organised by some careers advisers to explain their position to careers coordinators and senior staff. The annual review of the Service Level Agreement provided a good opportunity to have this discussion. In very supportive schools therefore, this worked well and careers advisers could enlist their support, but some schools were less cooperative and other methods had to be found in order to gain the access they needed.

From our experience, many careers advisers are nervous about getting involved in curriculum related work, since they recognise their lack of knowledge in this area, and therefore feel unable to exert much influence on schools. We had to provide regular reassurance to help colleagues persevere and succeed with their enquiries.

During the Programme

Individual advisers developed a wide range of skills from being involved in the programme and from engaging in development work for their portfolio. For example, learning to plan and consult before rushing in too quickly was a vital part of colleagues' professional growth. The programme also provided a discipline which motivated colleagues to initiate change. Patrick, for example, said:

'I have been working in this school for nearly two years and... every week, like a ritual, I would mention the development of the resource centre to the careers coordinator. With doing the course I could no longer pay lip service to this area, but I actually had to do something about it.'

He included 'before and after' photographs in his portfolio, to show what he had achieved in this area. Another adviser, Gill, used the reflective action planning process to help resolve her tendency of starting projects without properly evaluating and concluding them. This process also helped her in prioritising, selecting and focusing more effectively on her professional interests.

Di recognised the importance of networking with other teachers in her school as a means of gaining their commitment and support for the work she wanted to do. There is a tendency for careers advisers to limit their contact with staff in schools, mainly because it is time consuming to network, and because they have very pressing schedules to meet their target numbers of guidance interviews and group sessions. However, this programme serves to reinforce the fact that advisers must involve others, if they are to influence the quality of the school's CEG curriculum.

The course has also encouraged some participants to involve themselves in aspects of careers work which they have hitherto avoided, such as cross-curricular work. This module was seen as rather daunting and time consuming, although Patrick has subsequently proceeded to lead a county project in this area as a result of expertise gained from this course and commented, 'My own knowledge in this area has also grown… and I am even finding colleagues asking my advice about this area of work, which has helped to boost my self confidence'.

All the careers advisers found the module on guidance and support the easiest to tackle, since it linked most closely to their specialist area of work. Anu found this module a useful resource on which to base his discussion with his careers teachers: 'I found it useful to look at the different approaches to organising interviews. I have brought up these points with both my careers teachers, which has led to some healthy debate about access'.

In one instance, a careers adviser and a teacher from one her schools were both following the course at the same time. They began working separately, but slowly, and with our encouragement, they started to work on it together. Meetings were convened once a week and they planned jointly which areas to tackle. Development tasks were divided up and ideas and suggestions were generated for action. In this way, they were constantly reviewing their progress together and providing each other with feedback on their enquiry tasks. This model is an excellent example of how joint training of careers advisers and careers teachers can benefit careers work in school. Both of them found the mutual support encouraging and challenging.

On Completion

Having completed the programme, all of the careers advisers shared the sort of sentiment expressed by Colette:

> 'Unless you can get involved in developing things then you just end up going through the motions. Refreshing yourself on the theory is okay, but without developments taking place it just becomes an academic, paper exercise and can get very tedious.'

Undertaking the programme has helped this group to recognise which of their schools are willing and able to support them in developing careers work and which are not. This has meant working on different aspects of their careers work programme with a number of schools. Growth in self-confidence and assertiveness has been quite marked, and has increased practitioners' feelings of professional competence. Patrick said:

> 'I feel that I could now walk into a resource centre and look at the layout and the information it contained and be able to comment on it and perhaps make some suggestions if it were needed. I would not have felt this confident before completing the workbook.'

Confidence to relate to other members of the teaching staff was also highlighted by Anu:

'My main channel of communication before starting the course was to snatch brief discussions with the careers teacher; I didn't have any contact with other members of staff. One year on, I now have regular monthly meetings with the careers team to discuss new issues and developments. I have more contact with staff. Not only am I approaching them, but they now contact me for help and advice.'

Gill expressed concern about what might happen to the developments she had initiated:

'In all honesty I am not sure how much of a chance of survival all these changes have... it seems to be me wanting to change and develop things and getting other people interested (this course has had something to do with this!), but if I were to leave the school tomorrow would it still continue? Would there be any review or evaluation? I would hope so.'

Overall, however, there is no doubt that by undertaking this programme, the careers advisers have been helped to fulfil a more active role in developing careers work with schools. All of them now know and deal with a wider range of people within their schools and all are more confident about tackling developments in relation to careers education and guidance. Although the programme has involved hard work, both for the advisers and the tutors, it really has made a difference as demonstrated by the following extracts from colleagues' portfolios.

'I really believe that I have moved on a great deal during the course of the year. I am no longer afraid to talk about and air my views on most aspects of careers education and guidance. The course has helped to increase my confidence in careers work.'

'I believe I am respected more by my schools and colleagues through the developments I have tried to implement over the last year.'

'I had the Records of Achievement Coordinator come up to me the other day to ask my advice!'

Although this particular course has been mainly used elsewhere by teachers, this group of careers advisers has shown that there is a need for post-experience training which helps them to relate their work in schools more closely with professional needs and concerns of the school community. This means making sense of the school network and becoming a recognised part of it. It also means developing effective channels of communication through to senior managers, so that careers advisers can be seen as an important resource to the school, and not someone with competing priorities and concerns. Through the process of professional enquiry and reflection (a necessary part of the portfolio), careers advisers have had to consult much more broadly; to ask questions, suggest action and evaluate practice. This has demonstrably benefited them as individuals, but it has also shown teacher colleagues that careers advisers too are concerned with developing professional practice in a robust and pragmatic way. This has to contribute to building dialogue, professional respect and personal trust. Future opportunities for joint training must now the be next step in forging still stronger partnerships between the new Careers Services and schools.

CHAPTER 14

CASE STUDIES IN THE DEVELOPMENT OF CAREERS EDUCATION

Hilary Harber, Emma Hewitt and Gillian Bannister

This chapter illustrates the kind of impact that professional development schemes can have when they set out to be directly supportive of school improvement. The three case studies included here provide detailed insight into the process of change and show how the improvement of individual teachers can not only transform the provision of CEG but also have a major impact on the school as an organisation. These accounts also provide a clear view of the operation of the Careers Work Training Partnership operating in East Sussex, Surrey and Staffordshire and tell us a great deal about professional development issues.

Case Study A: Hilary Harber

Careers Coordinator, Oxted County School, Surrey; 11–18 mixed comprehensive

I began working on material for the Advanced Certificate in Careers Education and Guidance in October 1993 and completed my portfolio in January 1995. One of the key benefits of the course has been its emphasis on good planning and evaluation; the *process* of project implementation is just as important as the content. To some extent this makes the lessons learned more lasting and far reaching. Thus, this summative reflection that forms the final section of my portfolio seemed a natural and vital part of the whole process.

I embarked upon the course new to the post of Careers Coordinator, knowing relatively little about the scope of the job I had agreed to undertake. The last four terms have been the busiest of my professional life. I have had to learn fast as I have been exposed to a number of new situations. Frequently I have been involved with collaborative work that has developed my communication and management skills. I signed up to the careers work course hoping that it would help me with my new responsibilities. It has achieved that and a lot more.

Development Tasks

During the year I initiated a number of developments covering the six key areas of careers work. I shall describe three of the tasks which illustrate the nature of the work undertaken.

1. Cross-curricular Careers Work

Messages about careers can become confused and uncoordinated if subject teachers are not aware of or in sympathy with the school's policy on careers education and guidance (CEG). I soon realised that I was not fully aware of all the cross-curricular activities relating to careers work that were operating in the school. I decided to carry out a cross-curricular audit in order to identify the type of careers work carried out by subject teachers in all departments.

I wrote to each head of department briefly explaining the purpose of the audit and the main aims of CEG. I used the DOTS (Decision making skills: Opportunity awareness: Transition learning: Self-awareness) model to widen their understanding of careers work since I believe that many teachers regard it simply as the provision of job information. The audit was carried out through personal interviews with each department head and divided into two parts. In part one I asked whether or not the department covered each of the nine topics:

- career concepts and ideas;
- work concepts and ideas;
- people, careers and work;
- controversial issues in careers and work;
- self awareness for career and work;
- opportunity awareness;
- personal work experiences;
- personal career planning;
- career changes and transitions.

The results of part one were easily displayed in a matrix. In part two I made assumptions about the type of careers work that each department might practise. This led to lengthy discussions about the tasks which departments already undertake and those which they may consider trying. In this way I could identify not only discrete activities but also approaches that infuse the curriculum.

The task of interviewing 18 department heads seemed daunting. Indeed, it became very time consuming since each interview was at least 30 minutes long. However the responses to my initial approaches were invariably positive; some were very open to discussion while others had very fixed views about the delivery of their subject and were resistant to any potential 'imposition'.

I found that already a lot of cross-curricular careers work was being delivered. Some departments were contributing without realising. My main recommendations were (1) to encourage departments to improve the quality of their careers work, and (2) to raise the issue of the paucity of personal career planning with senior management.

I discussed the results of the audit with the senior teacher responsible for staff development. He was very supportive of my suggestion that there was a need for staff in-service training on CEG. I had only recently become aware of the wide scope of CEG and it therefore seemed likely that all staff could benefit from an awareness raising exercise, since we all have a responsibility to deliver CEG. I was invited to put my proposal for a cross-curricular themes INSET day to the development committee. Their reaction was mixed, largely because departments are overburdened with national curriculum matters. A cross-curricular rather than a departmental INSET day seemed to be creating extra pressure. A compromise was agreed: one representative from each department would attend a careers training session for half a day. The feedback has been positive and I look forward to reviewing the developments that each department is undertaking with year 7.

2. Community-linked Work

I attended a TVEI(E) training day entitled 'Widening horizons through work-related activities'. The initiative being promoted seemed an appropriate one to develop as one of my community-linked tasks. In conjunction with the school's Special Educational Needs Coordinator (SENCO), I identified a realistic set of outcomes for our project. We aimed to develop, use and evaluate activities that challenge the narrow and stereotypical attitudes of year 10 SEN pupils as they prepared to select their work experience placements.

An action plan was drawn up. The SENCO developed a sequence of six lessons for the SEN pupils. An English teacher supported by the SENCO also used the material with a low ability year 11 class. The lessons were most successful. Pupils usually reluctant to express any opinion enjoyed participating in a 'What's my line?' game. One outcome of this was that pupils highlighted *for themselves* the need to undertake careers research. Once a focus for each pupil's research had been established, they were allowed to undertake the research in the careers library. Not only did the pupils gain more knowledge about a range of careers relevant to their future plans but they also developed their information handling skills with a variety of media. Their final piece of work was wordprocessed, improving their IT skills.

The most gratifying aspect of this development has been the way in which other colleagues were drawn in by the success of the idea. The relevance of the work was a strong motivational force. The pupils were, for once, proud of their final articles and had completed more confidently the oral element of the course. The self-esteem of a fairly disaffected group of year 11 pupils was raised. Other English teachers are now aware of the potential of using the careers library. I shall build into the year 10 careers lessons elements of this project in an attempt to widen the horizons of all pupils as they prepare for work experience.

3. Recording, Reporting and Reviewing

Initially my aim was to develop a form which year 9 pupils would complete with the guidance of their tutor as they completed their spring term careers projects. The projects were designed to help the pupils to make more informed GCSE option choices. It seemed appropriate to find a way of recording the pupils' career development progress and to invite them to justify their option choices. The tutors implemented the form with success.

Having identified a need to improve the provision of personal career action planning, I wondered if I could develop a personal target-setting scheme that encouraged pupils to record and reflect upon their achievements. I suggested the idea to my colleague who had recently been appointed to the new post of tutorial programme coordinator. By the end of the summer term we had agreed a format for a target-setting programme that would be introduced to each year group. Four skills were selected: working independently, working with other people, making transitions and decision making. Using a prompt list, pupils described what they had done to demonstrate their ability in these areas. One area in need of development was selected by the pupil and in consultation with peers and the tutor an achievable target could be set and later reviewed.

We introduced the plan to heads of house and, rather hurriedly, to the tutors at the start of the new academic year. With hindsight we realise that we were naive in hoping to launch such a scheme across the whole school (60 tutors) with so little time to explain the programme. We have learned that it would have been wiser to pilot the material with a small team of willing tutors. This would have identified weaknesses in the paperwork (content and presentation) and would have allowed us to give more time to support the tutors who were all unfamiliar with the process.

There have been a number of notable outcomes following the introduction of the tutorial programme coordinator and the target-setting scheme. In addition to the vertically organised house meetings, there has been a need for tutors to meet in year groups. A review of the tutorial system is now taking place. It is likely that more time will be allocated to tutorials. The introduction of a programme that addressed the needs of each year group was a key factor in the instigation of a pastoral training day. The whole staff has recently examined the role that the tutor plays in improving and supporting the learning process. We look forward to further developments in this area.

Evaluating the Careers Work Course

In order to evaluate my experience of the careers work course I think it is helpful to identify both the costs and the benefits.

Costs

Time. This was undoubtedly the major cost incurred in a number of ways. First, the tasks in the workbooks required quiet reflective time in order to respond meaningfully to the case studies. It is possible to write quick answers but this results in the main learning points of the exercise either being missed or quickly forgotten. Secondly, the development tasks themselves take time at all stages: planning, development, implementation and evaluation. The amount of time required varied from task to task and it is not possible to specify the length of time involved. I initiated ten development tasks which each probably took between about 5 hours and 15 hours to complete.

Finally, I held a large number of consultation meetings with my mentor and all the other staff with whom I have worked collaboratively in order to implement the developments. Most of these meetings probably would not have happened if I had not been following the course.

Extra paperwork. The course has generated a lot of extra paperwork: recording my thoughts in a journal, writing action plans and reflective commentaries. Despite all the extra work entailed, I am surprised at how enjoyable the reflective writing for each part of the course has been and I am pleased that my IT skills have improved.

Challenging the status quo. The course has introduced me to new ideas; it has widened the scope of my job and encouraged me to undertake developments which have challenged the comfortable status quo. Since most careers work involves colleagues I have had to cope with change not only for myself but also with other staff. I have learned that they need to be consulted at an early stage so that they are as ready for the change as I am.

Feeling overwhelmed. There was always a danger of feeling overwhelmed by the number of tasks that I needed to tackle. There were times when I found it hard to keep up with the pace of change. The school calendar dictated when each initiative must be delivered which, to some extent, accounted for a sense of feeling unable to control my own work. The course made me more aware of how much work there is to do in the careers department; there was a danger of being depressed by this unless I reminded myself that I would get there one step at a time. This advice also encourages one to recognise that we cannot always reach the ideal in the short term; that is something to aim at over several years.

To sum up, this course has caused me to undertake more work. Through working harder I have learned how to work more effectively and have gained a tremendous sense of satisfaction.

Benefits

Scope of CEG. I started with a fairly limited view of my role: managing work experience, organising year 11 interviews, planning and delivering careers lessons in PSE and resourcing the careers library. The workbooks have expanded that view. I now recognise the importance of cross-curricular careers work and the responsibility that it places on me to make all staff in the school aware of the changes that have taken place in CEG. I feel that my management skills have been challenged in a number of ways. For example, I am now encouraging colleagues to take on part of the responsibility for delivering CEG in their roles of tutor *and* subject teacher. This requires a carefully planned approach. The area that has surprised me most is recording, reporting and reviewing. I have been involved in starting a target-setting scheme which seems to me to be at the heart of the educational process.

I also see that my function is not simply to organise careers interviews but to support the interview process; work experience is only one type of contact with the community; and the careers library must be made more accessible and better known by all staff and pupils. Not only has the course opened my eyes but it has also given me clearer objectives and strategies for achieving my targets.

Educational theories. It has been a while since I have done any theoretical educational reading. While I am aware that I could have read more, it has been good to return to this. Having been a practising teacher for six years, I have been able to appreciate the theoretical perspectives on education that now seem more useful and underpin the way a good teacher operates.

Quality of the materials. I have been impressed with the careers work workbooks which were easy to read although the responses do require time. Sometimes the language or structure of matrices was not helpful but it was never difficult to adapt the material. Theories of career development can appear to over-simplify the processes. I found it helpful to consider the models as they do improve our understanding of the way children build up a picture of the world of work and how they fit into it.

The exercises formed a part of the evidence which was particularly important where enquiry rather than development took place. As I reflected on each section I found the introduction of each book an invaluable reminder of all the key issues covered.

Professionalism. I know that my own confidence and professionalism have increased during the last year. The course has encouraged a systematic and thoughtful approach to every stage of the development cycle: thinking, planning, refining, implementing and evaluating. The emphasis placed on evaluation has reminded me that everything can always be refined and improved. Change is something that one should not only expect but also desire. The process of continual change might seem threatening but it seems to me that if it is carried out at a manageable and appropriate pace it is the only way to ensure progress.

I am more assertive. This has come from a more secure understanding of my reasons for undertaking each development. I am clearer about what I need to achieve and how others can assist. I am more sure of my own ground and have a stronger sense of purpose.

OFSTED. In March 1994 the school was inspected. I know that the work that I had completed for the course gave me the best possible preparation for the inspection. I found that I enjoyed the interview since I had a well-prepared handbook. I knew what I wanted to say about each area of careers work and could confidently discuss my plans for evaluating the course. It was frustrating not to receive any personal feedback during the week of inspection.

Satisfaction. I have gained a tremendous sense of satisfaction from seeing developments underway in all seven areas of the course. Other staff have shared in this too since the PSHE team are now delivering a better set of careers lessons. Working with other staff has been both rewarding and challenging. The cross-curricular audit brought me into contact with 18 heads of department; it was exciting to discover just how much was already going on and to be able to build on that. I have also learned through the frustration of working with colleagues whose aims are not always allied to my own.

Meeting other careers coordinators. This has been useful since we all share very similar concerns. Few members of staff within school could appreciate the issues that we discussed at our group meetings.

Profile and impact of CEG. The profile of CEG in the school has been raised. My mentor, who is a deputy head, the PHSE teams, the tutor teams, heads of department and the staff development committee have all been involved in some of the developments and are more aware of the scope of CEG. I am particularly pleased to have won half an INSET day to develop cross-curricular careers work.

In conclusion, I know that both the school and the pupils have gained from my participation in this course because of the impact of all the development tasks. The course has worked for my own personal benefit too; I am more confident and have developed professionally. I do not begrudge any of the hours spent because the benefits have far outweighed the costs and have been so plain to see.

Case Study B: Emma Hewitt

Careers Coordinator, Varndean Sixth Form College, East Sussex

My role at Varndean Sixth Form College is to coordinate careers education and guidance. I undertook the Careers Work certificate course because I wanted to improve my skills and knowledge, develop my confidence in the role and improve the status of CEG within the college.

The Value of an Accredited Programme

The main reason I was attracted to the open learning course was that it would allow me to undertake professional development in conjunction with my current responsibilities, not in addition to them. When working through the workbooks I found that I could directly link and apply the results to what I am aiming to achieve in the college. The flexibility of the programme was also very attractive in that it allowed me to work at my own pace and direct the focus of my development work.

The result of the curriculum development I have initiated is that the nature of careers education and guidance within the college has become more proactive and an integral part of the whole college curriculum. Through my developmental initiatives, many of the ideas and concepts put forward have become central to many cross-college initiatives; for example, the use of individual action plans for formative purposes. At the outset, I was conscious that the course should lead to tangible benefits for the institution. I thus needed to base my research on 'real' issues, addressing practical questions.

Action Planning for Improvement

I was very new to the role as Careers Coordinator and did not have any significant previous learning, so most of the work was completely new to me. I was able to clearly identify areas for development through interaction with the workbooks, I read each of the workbook units before attempting to produce action plans. My action plans for each section clarified the starting point for each unit. For example, before reflecting upon classroom work I decided to familiarise myself with all the different ways in which careers education can be delivered, only then did I feel that I had the relevant knowledge and expertise with which to reflect on current practice. I collected data using audits adapted from the Careers Work materials; I also had both formal and informal conversations with colleagues and mentors. I included records of data collection at the end of each section of my portfolio and kept a journal containing relevant learning, ideas and experiences. Reflection on, and analysis of, the data was based on criteria outlined in the workbooks and the results of need and climate analysis within the institution. Action strategies flowed from this analysis. The conclusion to each section of my portfolio provided an outline of the development I had initiated and reflection on how these initiatives have been implemented and received.

My overall development was the result of questioning existing practice; a process which I began with the activities in the 'Starting Points' workbook. I evaluated what I considered to be the strengths and weaknesses of the current provision, and then drew up a tentative list of basic areas that I considered warranted further investigation. The questions I asked were based on ideas that I encountered in the workbooks. I found that in many cases what used to work no longer did, which I realised through research, as a result of a response to a changed environment. My resource centre work questionnaire illustrated that the system for arranging a careers interview was no longer working effectively and therefore a new system had to be devised.

Adapting 'Careers Work' for the 16–19 Context

The workbooks seemed to be designed for use by staff in 11–18 schools rather than colleges like mine, so I had to adapt many of the activities. Although time consuming, I do feel that it has been useful in broadening my understanding of careers work with the pre-16 age range, and this is important in terms of my own professional and career development as well as enabling me to see our work in relation to what students may have experienced in their high schools.

Working with the Careers Adviser

This curriculum development work has been needs-driven, resulting from enquiry on my part and collaboration with others, most notably the careers adviser based at the college. Discussion of ideas with her has been of considerable help. It has been useful for me to have input from someone who is operating on a different agenda so that an element of objectivity is introduced.

Managing Change through Evaluation

Throughout this professional development I have been able to reflect on the process of change. Developing a theoretical perspective was vital in that it gave me an overview and helped me to analyse the process of development. It highlighted specific issues that need to be addressed by any initiator of change. The Managing Careers Work unit was particularly useful in this respect. A change that I feel has made a worthwhile difference to students has been the operation of 'carousels' introducing students to the careers resource base and the interactive computer databases. 'Resisting erosion' has also been demonstrated in the development of career action plans. They have been fully integrated into the tutorial programme and, because they have been viewed as an important new feature, they are now regularly timetabled into the programme.

I feel that the success of a development can really only be assessed later, so I intend to re-evaluate these improvements in the next stage of the programme. The careers education modules we developed this year will need to be completely re-evaluated before they are put into operation next year. The carousels and action plans could only be viewed as successful at the point where students submitted UCAS and employment applications that were obviously a result of more effective and detailed research and planning. The checklist that I designed for UCAS applicants was very successful and this year it has been updated and issued to all potential applicants.

Managing the process of change, requires careful and considered planning and implementation, but must also be sensitive to constraints and inhibitors. The inhibitors may often come from staff, so effective communication is the key to establishing common ground. It is also important to establish common ground with students since acceptance by them will help ensure impact and survivability. I ensured that the audit of cross-college career themes was clearly explained so that department heads did not see it as a time-wasting activity, but one that could result in tangible benefits for the students. This has been important in encouraging them to update their Records of Achievement. I wrote and disseminated a list of reasons why they should update and the response has been far more positive this year.

I have taken care to produce sound evidence to support proposals for change. For example I designed a checklist for the UCAS process including information on recent changes. This is used by students in conjunction with their tutors. Colleagues are willing to use the resources I produce because they know that they are underpinned by systematic enquiry. Also, colleagues do not feel threatened when I suggest strategies for change, since they appreciate that it will have been carefully considered and likely to be an improvement on previous practice.

Working with the Organisation

Managing change also required me to consider at the outset the college's professional culture and organisational structure: the beliefs, attitudes and behaviours which prevail. Much of the development I have initiated has been facilitated by the tacit support of colleagues and students. It is important to involve both teachers and students in the process and this is reflected throughout most of the audits I undertook of current practice, in resource-centre, classroom, cross-curricular and community-linked work. I consciously considered it in any strategies for change. I asked students through a questionnaire how they rated the current careers resource base, and how user friendly and useful it was for them. I also asked for their suggestions for improvement, many of which have been implemented. Staff were asked to respond on the INSET session as well as being asked how we could further support them in their tutor role, and other ideas for improvement. By asking for feedback the department has been able to ensure that it is best serving those it is designed to support.

I have also needed to be aware of the college's long-term development plan: improving quality of provision across the college is one of its central themes as stated in the Further Education Funding Council (FEFC) circular 93/28, 'Colleges need to find time to develop an incremental approach to quality. This means devising and implementing coherent and carefully placed strategies that establish quality as everyone's responsibility.' For development to be successful it must fit in with college wide initiatives and respond to them. Throughout the development I have had continuous support from the senior management team so I have been able to make important decisions without interference from above. I have a regular meeting with the vice-principal responsible for guidance which has been of great importance because he can offer advice and has the ability to make things happen. I felt it was important for example, that, when I drafted the paper proposing a cross-college work experience team, his name was associated with it so that it could gain the credence it required.

I identified the need for staff INSET because I felt that it was vital to ensure support from my colleagues before implementing new structures and procedures. I needed to communicate to tutors that I felt that the work that they were already doing was being done well so that the session would been seen as progressive. It would be an opportunity for them to respond to externally driven forces and thereby improve the quality of careers education and guidance they were offering their students.

Reflecting on Progress

When referring back to the aims and objectives outlined in my original development plan, I can confidently report that I have met all of them and initiated other developments not anticipated at the time. My own professional development has been considerable. My knowledge and understanding of careers work has improved beyond recognition and I feel confident in my ability and skills as careers coordinator, and I think that I have been able to earn the respect of colleagues in this role.

I would like to be able to reflect on this portfolio in a year from now because so many of my initiatives and ideas are still embryonic. I would also like to consider how I have been able to use my new skills and knowledge in my developing role in the college. It is important that the college has a suitably qualified person in the role of careers coordinator, and I am glad that I have been able to fulfil this. Careers work in schools and colleges is too often coordinated by people who have no training (as identified in a recent National Association of Careers and Guidance Teachers (NACGT) report), so if the profile and status of this type of work is to be raised then it is very important that qualified staff are in position.

Future Developments

The process of systematic enquiry and portfolio development has helped me to set targets for future development as follows.

- Develop a whole college careers education and guidance policy. Much of the groundwork has already been done as part of this course, but it now needs to be followed up and consolidated into a comprehensive framework.
- Fully utilise the *Coordinating Careers Work* pack, (Law *et al*, 1991b). I now have the knowledge and understanding to be able to carry out the practical exercises and it will be a very useful starting point for developing a college policy.
- Question students, on exit, as to the effectiveness and value they attribute to the careers education and guidance received at college. Value-added analysis is politically important and I do not see why it should only be applicable to academic progress. A questionnaire would also allow us to identify weakness in our current provision.

Conclusion

This course has given me the opportunity to make sense of past experience, to learn from the open learning programme and consequently to initiate curriculum development. I have thoroughly enjoyed compiling my portfolio and I am very proud of what I have produced. I am pleased that I will be able to use it during a FEFC cross-college inspection in March as I am sure that it will be useful documentation illustrating the quality of careers provision at the college.

I found that the group sessions were very useful. They helped me to meet with people who were experienced in the role of careers coordinator. We gave each other ideas and mutual support. I was sad when one member of the group temporarily withdrew and I would want to encourage her to complete this course since, if she learns as much as I have, she will find it very beneficial. My local support tutor has given me a wealth of materials and provided me with the vital encouragement I needed. She was very thorough in her interim assessment in June, and her suggestions were extremely helpful. My mentors have been invaluable too. They have both provided me with support and encouragement. I am glad that I chose two people, since the careers adviser has been able to give me expert help and the vice-principal has been able to help me with the feasibility of institutional development.

Case Study C: Gillian Bannister

Careers Coordinator, Cannock Chase High School, Staffordshire

I was a careers coordinator at Cannock Chase High School and responsible for careers education and guidance when I became a participant in the accredited Careers Work course. Towards the end of my course I was asked to give a talk to a new group just starting and this gave me a useful opportunity to reflect on the process I had been through. Giving the talk was, for me, a useful way to work out some of what I wanted to say in the summative reflection section of my portfolio.

One of my interests is walking in the Lake District. I enjoy the planning of the route and the walk itself, but I find no compulsion to stand on the summit when I arrive. Even before I have finished one walk I am thinking about and planning the next. My journey with the portfolio has been rather similar, and, just as I needed a good map and companion to help me keep my spirits up, with the portfolio I needed positive guidance to actually complete the course.

I felt comfortable with the process once the light had finally dawned and I now incorporate the system of evaluating, action planning and reflecting into my teaching style. It was useful, for example, to be reminded of how important it is to carry out an audit. Also, it became clear to me that, all too often, I have been functioning automatically; dealing with situations as I thought they were, rather than as they really were. Putting myself through the Careers Work course has helped me to realise that, although I have preferred styles of management and learning, to be efficient and productive, I must draw on a variety of styles.

When looking back through the portfolio, it appears at first to be rather formal, not really me, but, when I read more closely I can see that the portfolio allowed me to express my sense of humour too – an essential ingredient in curriculum development. On the down side, I know I could have spent more time 'dressing to impress' and I still have work to do to compensate for my poor spelling and wordprocessing skills. By completing all of the Careers Work sections, I was able to develop an excellent overview and gather a good body of evidence which will be helpful in the future when the senior management team need convincing that development in careers education is essential.

Because I have been able to develop a clear rationale for careers education and guidance and have some impact within the school, many of my colleagues now realise that the careers train is certainly one to be aboard, because we go to exciting places, do interesting things, and, most important, careers education and guidance underpins good learning in the school. My original reason for starting the course was the imminence of an OFSTED inspection; I used it as a framework for enquiry, guiding me through the process of informing myself about the state of affairs in all the obvious careers related areas. I feel we are now more prepared, and it is satisfying to see that careers is now firmly established on the school development plan.

One of the things I discovered was that I knew very little about the Careers Service functions and so I was able to plan ways of addressing this with work shadowing and other awareness-raising activities. The course has provided an avenue for my own professional development, an opportunity which is now opening up for others in the school. My experience has been a good preparation for supporting others and I am now mentor to a colleague who has started the course this year. Some less effective aspects of my professional performance have become more obvious during the course – struggling to meet deadlines and not making full use of my mentors for example. More positively however, my confidence and enthusiasm have developed and the support from colleagues and Careers Service staff have kept me going.

One of the major lessons I have learnt by doing this course is that CEG should not be the concern of a single person in the school and so I have decided to relinquish my role as the sole coordinator in order to enable several colleagues to become involved. This will lead, I hope, to a more whole school approach. The way forward for me is to share my knowledge, expertise and enthusiasm with others, so that careers education and guidance can be delivered at some level by everyone. My talk to the new group was important for me because I felt that I was doing my bit to encourage others and help them to get off to a good start on a challenging but exciting journey. So here are the cards I used in my talk and some of the comments I made about them.

Figure 14.1 Survival kit

**1. Get aboard
the mystery train**

When you get aboard the mystery
train you need to be ready for
anything. It is in the nature of
development work that you cannot
predict when you will learn or how
the implementation of change will
turn out.

**2. The dangers of
too many hats**

When you tackle development work
systematically you may find yourself
getting involved in multiple
initiatives. The key is to be careful
with your action plans. Be realistic
with your targets and time scales.

3. A planning system

You really need a good planning
system so that you can see at a glance
where you are in the process. Good
planning will save you a lot of stress
in the long run.

4. Don't fall at the first hurdle

The first time you submit your
portfolio for assessment can seem
challenging, but ongoing assessment
will sharpen the focus of what you
are doing and it is helpful to have
stages to the process. Try to avoid
getting too attached to your portfolio
– let others in on what is going on.

5. Bags of perseverance

Open learning is a hard road and
you will probably need to dip into
your bags of perseverance quite
often. Your mentor and tutors will
help to top up your bags when they
get low, but you must not forget that
they need some too. So try to top
theirs up from time to time with
some encouraging words.

**6. What kind of worker
are you?**

You will need to know what kind of
a worker you really are. Start by
reflecting on your strengths and
weakness and make adjustments to
your working habits where
appropriate.

7. Have floppy, will travel

Always carry your portfolio around
on a floppy disc so that you can
make a bit of progress whenever you
can grab a little time. But, don't
forget to back it up as soon as you
touch base – floppies can get
corrupted and you could lose
everything.

8. Eventually the light dawns

When you first get started everything
seems hazy and you feel perpetually
in the dark. Don't worry, the light
will eventually dawn – and when it
does the illumination is dazzling.

9. How do you travel?

We are all different in the way we deal with a journey. You need to know what kind of traveller you really are, what keeps you going and what will help you to find your way. Think about it deliberately and write it down. The portfolio is there to help you reflect and work these things out.

10. It's good to talk

Keep in touch with your group; they will help to keep you going when the going gets tough. Open learning does not have to be a lonely and isolated affair.

11. Legwork is important

Effective development work means meeting people. Change does not take place in isolation and it is important to 'talk-up' CEG in as many areas as possible. Be prepared to act as a bridge between the various people who need to be involved in initiatives.

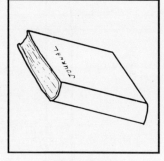

12. Keep a journal

Keep a journal or diary and make regular entries – every day if you can. This will help you to monitor progress, spread the workload and will give you a lot of information when it is time to produce a report or collect evidence for your portfolio.

13. Update your IT skills

Computer skills are essential for
portfolio development but, these
days, any professional activity is
impoverished without them, so if
you have not yet learned to use a
wordprocessor, now is the time to
start.

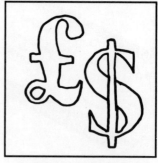

14. Bribery and corruption?

Change and development affect
colleagues in a personal way. You
may need to oil the wheels
sometimes and pay attention to
colleagues' sensitivities. Bribery may
be taking things too far, but try to
think of what you can offer to
compensate for what colleagues
think they might be losing.

**15. Hard hats must be worn
at all times**

Change and development can lead to
a backlash of criticism and even
resentment. Be prepared to take all
reasonable measures to protect
yourself. You may have a hard hat
and a flak jacket but, in the end, you
just have to toughen up.

The editors would like to thank Kyra Atkin for additional artwork.

CHAPTER 15

THE ROLE OF CAREERS EDUCATION IN SOCIAL RENEWAL

David Cleaton and Lesley Arnold

Our experience of running a careers education and guidance training programme for a wide range of professionals in the small Indian Ocean state of Seychelles, has provided us with a rather exceptional opportunity to reflect on the important role which careers education and guidance (CEG) plays in the development of a healthy economy and how it can contribute to a changing national culture. Our training course acted as a microcosm within which some of the social and economic issues facing the Seychelles were highlighted. It also helped us to explore not only the purpose of CEG, but its role in raising the consciousness of all professionals who are in a position to affect change within that society.

Some Background

Our first contact with the Seychelles arose when Sussex University asked for a representative from East Sussex Careers Services to speak to a group of overseas students about the British system of careers guidance. A strong link between the university and the Seychelles already existed, and our connection with them developed as we subsequently provided work placements for Seychelles students in our careers centres.

It was clear to us that the state of careers guidance in these Indian Ocean islands was somewhat impoverished. There was little or no local careers information and very limited careers resources, largely imported from the UK. The Seychelles Ministry of Administration and Management (MAM) sent an official, Edwina Adrienne, to undertake a three-week placement with East Sussex Careers Service and this led to a request for us to provide a training course for careers teachers and advisers in the Seychelles, along the lines of the standards operational in East Sussex Careers Services.

This proposal was later to become part of a national plan for human resource development. The government of Seychelles wanted to be released from a dependency on expatriate labour which was associated with skill shortages on the one hand, and surplus labour on the other. There was a definite recognition, in this context, of the potential economic value to be gained through improving the quality of careers education and guidance.

Being in a period of transition, Seychelles is rapidly shifting from an economy with a central direction and state ownership to one relying increasingly on private initiative and market mechanisms. This process of transition is well under way but now poised at a very critical stage, as the economy labours under a range of well-known handicaps, one of the major being the human resource factor. We submitted a proposal for training which was accepted, and we prepared for Phase I of the course which was scheduled for July 1993. We were impressed by the fact that three government departments, the Ministry of Administration and Manpower – our contact ministry, the Ministry of Education and the Ministry of Employment and Social Affairs, collaborated to ensure that the training could take place.

The Design of the Training Programme

We hoped that the programme would enable the students to develop a knowledge and understanding of the principles of careers guidance and, most crucially, to help them develop the skills they would need to be able to develop further and support their own work after we had returned to the UK. As external trainers, we had complementary styles, strength and expertise. One of us had an extensive background in teaching and training in careers education and the other experience of training careers staff in individual guidance skills. Both of us had strong belief in the use of highly participative techniques and experiential learning. In our design of the programme we had included a wide range of practical sessions which would, hopefully, enable the participants to develop their own skills in producing careers material for use with their students. We also planned to enable them to develop the basic techniques for conducting one-to-one guidance interviews. Underpinning this would be input on the principles of careers guidance, and sessions which we hoped would enable them to reflect on the learning that had taken place. Above all, we wanted the course to be as relevant as possible to their work in Seychelles. A reliance on careers material related to the UK might be interesting but would not encourage the Seychellois to learn how to design and develop their own materials and begin to build up their own resources.

From our discussion with Edwina Adrienne we knew that the participants' experiences and expertise varied considerably; one fact was prominent – very few of them had ever undertaken much formal training. Some were teachers of long standing, although with little experience of teacher education. One or two had previously attended academic or vocational courses in countries with which the formerly Marxist Seychelles had established close links, such as Cuba and former East Germany. One teacher had completed the two-year BEd degree, which the University of Sussex had delivered on behalf of the Seychelles government, and had spent some time on placement at the Brighton and Hove Careers Centre in East Sussex. There would also be several staff from the Ministry of Employment who were working in the equivalent of our job centres, demonstrating the collaborative approach between the various government departments. We were therefore aware of the fact that the course participants represented a significant 'critical mass' within the professional class of the Seychelles.

In designing Phase I of the course, we aimed to ensure that students would:

- understand the principles of careers education and guidance;
- recognise the constituent parts of the process;
- agree a model which could support their practice;
- understand the role of guidance practitioners;
- have acquired the appropriate skills;
- be able to implement the delivery of careers guidance.

During the period of design and preparation, we entered into discussion with Canterbury Christ Church College, to see if accreditation for the course would be possible so that the participants, if successful, would have some form of recognised qualification.

Adapting to a Different Cultural Context

Clearly we also had concerns about the language ability of the course participants. We did not know until we arrived on Mahe that our students were trilingual and would have been equally at home had we delivered the course in French or Creole. However, we were teaching a course which was being delivered and assessed in English, a language which was not necessarily the students' mother tongue. This experience demonstrated the central role which language plays in any national development, and it is vital for 'external' trainers to consider the issues which arise from the context in which they are working. We had concerns about the level of understanding which course participants would have. Given what we knew about the history of the Seychelles and its traditional authoritarian and directive culture, we felt there were likely to be problems over such notions as 'client-centredness', 'non-directive counselling', or even 'choice'. Again, the reality was quite different. Most participants were able to relate quite quickly to these new concepts of 'helping skills'. Although the rate of acceptance varied, in general they understood the need for an eclectic approach to careers guidance.

Once we had secured, in principle, agreement for validation from the college, our concerns turned towards the participants' ability to study. Would they accept or adapt our methodology? Would they have sufficient time? What struck us both, was the high level of enthusiasm shown by all students. What they lacked in study skills they certainly made up for in enthusiasm, since public transport problems on the Seychelles are, to say the least, very difficult. Previous experience of training in cultures outside Western Europe suggested that we might encounter difficulties with a non-didactic approach to training. To an extent this was true, but the students quickly adapted to our participative style of delivery. The more we have worked with them, the more this is true.

The Structure of the Course

After the initial three-week taught course, which included a significant amount of assessable activities and reflection, we set the participants the task of producing monthly 'Review sheets'. These were collected by Edwina Adrienne and sent to the UK for our comments and observation. Each participant had to comment on the extent of their careers work during the previous month, describe what they had learnt and provide evidence of their involvement and achievement. In addition, during the time between the two taught phases of the course, each student was asked to explore their developing view of careers guidance in the form of a written paper.

In April 1994 we delivered the second phase of the course which lasted for two weeks. Of the 36 participants who completed the first taught phase, 32 continued with the second part of the programme. By the end of June 1994, all participants who wished to be considered for the Certificate in Careers Education and Guidance had to submit a portfolio of work providing evidence of their learning and professional development. This was achieved by 28 members of the group. After the portfolios were assessed, we conducted a tutorial with each participant during our third visit to the Seychelles in November 1994. During this tutorial each participant was asked to comment on their action-led research. To achieve the diploma, students had to complete an 8,000-word report that met the assessment criteria set by ourselves and the college; 25 of the students who had been awarded the certificate decided to aim for this qualification. Helping students complete their portfolios to the level required has not been without its problems. For example, lack of 'on site' resources meant that we had to take books and other resources with us. There were simply never enough to satisfy the needs of 30 students. There was also a lack of locally relevant documentation. Clearly, not everything could be transposed from the British scene. If sharing resources among 30 people was a problem, so too, was the need to give sufficient of our time to each person. A number of students lived and worked an hour's flight away, therefore contact during the evening was not possible. It also compounded the problems over sharing resources.

The absence of modern technological communication aids added further difficulties. Many of the teachers work in schools where photocopying is difficult, if not impossible and where overhead projectors are rare. Facsimile machines are non-existent in all of the schools.

Our experience also emphasises the problems we had in providing individual support from such a distance, and in monitoring students' progress between the two taught phases, especially where students were working on an individual 'action-centred research project' required for the diploma. This certainly added a new dimension to the concept of distance learning. Our links with Edwina Adrienne proved to be critical since she provided a coordinating role for students and a liaison role for us.

What Has Been Achieved?

Although this initial work will need to be developed and underpinned, early evidence does suggest that the training programme has produced outcomes of significant value, especially in terms of supporting these teachers in developing the knowledge and skills needed for them to undertake effective careers work with their students. This can be illustrated by reference to some of the case studies.

Case Study A: Joanne

This project looks at one way of improving women's participation in the labour market to enable them to become economically independent. Joanne becomes involved with a sewing training project which recruits women who are 'unemployed, school drop-outs, women who thought they had no future'. The training focuses on developing both sewing and business/entrepreneurial skills. She cites the enormous gains the women make in terms of confidence and business skills.

Case Study B: Marie

Marie addresses the issue of drop-out from work and education and its adverse links with productivity. She attributes this in part to a lack of resource material and constructs a set of work books which she argues will give CEG parity with other areas of the curriculum. In these materials, she addresses a range of issues, for example, the place of work in the family and the role of work in 'building the nation'.

Case Study C: Lars

Lars undertakes a survey of the careers information provision in a range of educational establishments. He identifies the fact that it is very varied in quality, quantity and value and that this is detrimental to students making effective career choices. While nationally the emphasis is on being flexible and taking active steps to seek employment or self-employment, there is very little in the schools, in terms of resources, to support this. He begins the process of updating careers information from his position in the manpower division.

Case Study D: Genvar

Genvar looks at the issues of gender stereotyping in relation to career choice, the reasons for this and the adverse effect this has on the economy. She surveys students on their motivation in subject areas and questions the impact of the teacher's gender on their success with the subjects. She interviews young women in non-stereotypical jobs and the parents of young women seeking non-stereotypical work. She also interviews employees on issues of bias in recruitment and devises case studies to challenge school students' ideas on job choice (jobs for boys and jobs for girls). She concludes with a list of recommendations which argue that women should be encouraged to consider the whole range of occupations and that not to do so is bad for the economy.

Case Study E: Lucy

Lucy looks at the importance of self-employment in the new Seychelles economy. She devises a set of lesson plans for students in secondary schools, both to encourage them to consider the option of self-employment and to give them some of the requisite skills to set up a business in agriculture, fishing or craft industries.

It has been particularly encouraging from our point of view to see the quality of evidence cited above, which students have documented from their work. However, there have also been other outcomes achieved throughout this partnership.

- The student group have successfully completed a three-week basic course in the theory and practice of careers guidance.
- Of these, 28 have achieved the standard of a Certificate in Careers Guidance, as accredited by Canterbury Christ Church College. This has been achieved by reaching the standards set for assessed individual work, an essay and a portfolio of over a year's duration.
- Of this group, 25 embarked upon an action-led research project which involved them in researching and writing an 8,000-word report.
- All of this has been reinforced by a commitment to careers guidance in the country's schools. This was underpinned by a one-day conference which we organised and delivered to 40 secondary school headteachers.
- The Seychelles government has recognised the importance of interdepartmental collaboration and cooperation in providing on-going support to schools. To this end, two of the participants have been seconded to the Ministry of Administration and Manpower. One of these colleagues comes from a teaching background and will adopt a role similar to that of an adviser for careers education. The other has a background in the media (journalist), as a reporter with the Seychelles Broadcasting Corporation, and is developing a careers information office. This colleague is about to embark upon a six-week placement with the East Sussex Careers Services.

- During each of our three visits to Seychelles, the government ministers involved in this venture have asked to be briefed and updated on the way things are progressing. This has presented us with an important opportunity to emphasise the points about a continuing commitment to careers guidance and its economic value and relevance.
- On our last visit we were asked to organise and deliver a two-day workshop for the staff of the Ministry of Employment (and Social Affairs) who work in the equivalent of our job centres.
- Almost every evening during our visits to Seychelles the careers issue has featured as a prime time evening news feature. This has emphasised to the general public the importance of careers guidance and the government's commitment to its development.

Future Possibilities

As far as we are concerned, we are reaching the end of the beginning. We have never experienced such a desire for knowledge and professional development as we have found amongst these careers guidance practitioners from the Seychelles. Already we are being asked about taking them into the next stage – further study for those willing and capable of going further. In conjunction with the teacher education department of the Seychelles Polytechnic, we are being asked to develop a programme of study in careers guidance for all trainee teachers. Whether we are the right trainers/consultants to take matters forward remains to be seen. However, we feel justly proud of what has been achieved, especially by the 36 'trainees' who gave up their annual holiday to spend three weeks in intensive tuition with us. Whatever the way forward, we will always remember the enthusiasm of those with whom we have worked. We believe we have helped build a platform on which development can progress.

Quality Assurance

This section provides guidance on quality
assurance approaches and the evaluation
of professional practice.

CHAPTER 16

QUALITY AND STANDARDS IN CAREERS WORK

Anthony Barnes

Background to the Current Interest in Quality and Standards

The current momentum to assess quality and standards in careers work in schools reflects a number of key influences. It is a feature of the wider move in education to improve outcomes for students. The Technical and Vocational Education Initiative Extension (TVEIE) devised measures of the impact of enhanced funding for careers education and guidance (CEG) on student outcomes. Other Employment Department initiatives, carrying funding for schools and Careers Services, have shown the same concern for 'value for money' indicators, with the emphasis on 'outcomes' rather than on 'processes'. In recent years, these initiatives have substantially increased the resources available for careers work, including the Careers Library initiative, the year 9 and 10 careers guidance initiative, the *Competitiveness* White Paper initiatives and (from the Department for Education) the Grant for Education Support and Training (GEST) to promote careers teacher training. Government departments are aware of the need to satisfy the scrutiny of the Treasury, auditors, ministers and other forms of public accountability for this additional resourcing.

This interest in quality and standards, should also be understood in the context of the culture and priorities of training and enterprise councils (TECs). Many TECs have funded local careers education and guidance initiatives often as part of their wider involvement in Youth Credits (formerly known as Training Credits), compacts, education-business link activities and their growing role in relation to the management of Careers Services. They have been persuaded of the important contribution that careers education and guidance can make to economic regeneration and, in particular, to the achievement of National Targets for Education and Training (NTETs). The notion of learning through life, expressed in terms of foundation and lifetime targets, reflects one of the central aims of careers education and guidance to promote students' awareness of lifelong learning as the key to lifelong career development. The aim of the new National Targets (May 1995) provide a powerful rationale for careers education and guidance:

'Developing Skills for a Successful Future'

Aim

To improve the UK's international competitiveness by raising standards and attainment levels in education and training to world class levels through ensuring that:

- all employers invest in employee development to achieve business success;
- all individuals have access to education and training opportunities, leading to recognised qualifications, which meet their needs and aspirations;
- all education and training develops self-reliance, flexibility and breadth, in particular through fostering competence in core skills.

Lifetime learning target three focuses on the need for organisations to become learning organisations which invest in the development of their human resources: '70% of all organisations employing 200 or more employees, and of those employing 50 or more, to be recognised as Investors in People.'

The Investors in People model of quality assurance has attracted TECs, LEAs and schools who have seen it as a way forward in developing staff, managing change, raising standards and contributing to a culture of continuous improvement. The influence of this approach with its emphasis on the four stages of commitment, planning, action and evaluation can be traced in some of the customised quality award schemes for CEG.

INVESTORS IN CAREERS
(Cornwall and Devon Careers Services)

To win the Investors in Careers Award, schools need to undergo a programme of assessment, meeting a performance standard in each of the four areas of commitment, planning, action and evaluation; and to achieve the following criteria:

1. release a teacher for a minimum of five days to undertake recognised training in careers education and guidance;
2. design a careers programme with specified measurable outcomes using the Evaluation Framework piloted by local teachers;
3. draw up service level agreements with local Careers Service staff to include specific contribution to group work with younger pupils;
4. provide final year students with data on the destinations and success rates of their immediate predecessors;
5. dissuade school leavers from making unrealistic post-16 choices or entering jobs without training;
6. involve employers and training providers in the curriculum.

Broadly, the current interest in securing quality and standards in CEG springs from two sources. One is to ensure accountability: to find ways of measuring the return on investment. The other is to ensure development: to provide a feedback loop so that those responsible for delivering quality receive an assessment of their progress to date, which they can use to plan further improvement. Most systems of quality assurance and inspection seek to achieve an appropriate balance between these two requirements and it is possible to locate individual schemes along the accountability–development continuum.

The Flexible Learning Perspective

Of particular interest to the theme of this book is the connection between the flexible learning perspective and schemes of quality assurance and inspection. It is more readily apparent in schemes which aim to promote internal review and development. This can be traced at three levels.

1. *Students.* Quality and standards may be related to student learning outcomes. One of the key outcomes for lifelong career development is the learning capability of students. Careers education and guidance should include flexible learning approaches so that students are equipped with the skills of managing their own learning and development.
2. *Teachers.* Flexible learning, through its emphasis on action planning and critical review, can help teachers to plan, deliver and evaluate CEG provision.
3. *Schools.* The school as an organisation can use feedback on its experience of providing careers education and guidance to plan further improvements.

Defining Quality in CEG

'Quality' is a difficult concept to pin down. It is intuitively understood in the context in which it is being used; but agreeing an operational definition is much more problematic. The meaning of the concept is further undermined by those who abuse it, in a marketing or public relations context, to describe a product or service which is anything but a quality one. Even schools and colleges, which in the past cultivated the image that their quality was self-evident, are now being challenged to demonstrate that they can substantiate their claims.

The starting point of quality is 'fitness for purpose' and reliable processes to meet agreed standards. In other words, the CEG provision must measure up to the aims and objectives laid down for it. Yet even this is a more complex issue than is first apparent because it begs the question, 'Who determines these aims and objectives and, therefore, has the power to decide what is meant by quality?' The concept of 'stakeholders' is very important in this issue of defining quality and is discussed later. However, even 'fitness for purpose' does not provide a complete definition of quality, because something which is fit for purpose could nevertheless be merely satisfactory or ordinary. Quality also carries with it the association of that which is excellent or distinctive, providing value for money and meeting high standards or even achieving perfection. Schemes to promote quality, therefore, may be about 'high' quality outcomes and not just about reliability in meeting agreed standards.

Once the stakeholders, who by definition have a vested interest in the outcomes of CEG, have devised operational criteria to measure 'quality', there is a choice of methods for monitoring and checking the level of quality. Broadly, these can be divided into *internal* and *external* assessment methods. Internal review and evaluation of CEG is regarded as the 'norm'; all schools and colleges ought to carry out their own monitoring, review and evaluation as a matter of course. For this, they will use a variety of instruments, such as questionnaires, surveys, interviews, reports and self-assessment proformas, such as quality assurance profiles. External review and evaluation by individuals or groups from outside the school, may be based on the use of similar instruments. The claim which is usually made to buttress the case for external review, is that it involves the objective application of the standards by an appropriate authority. This may or may not be true, depending on the credibility and competence of the authority and its methods. To motivate schools and colleges to achieve the standards, the process of quality assessment is sometimes developed into an award which may be loosely competitive and carry an appropriate incentive such as the promise of additional funding, or a scheme for public recognition of their achievement.

The Stakeholders' View of Quality

Any quality assurance or inspection system must try to strike a balance between the needs of all the stakeholders. There are different ways of categorising groups of stakeholders, but one of the most useful distinctions is between *internal* stakeholders (such as pupils and teachers) and *external* stakeholders (such as parents, governors, LEAs, TECs, Careers Services, business, the wider community and government).

It is fitting that students themselves should be identified as major stakeholders. There would be little purpose in having quality assurance schemes for CEG, if they did not put the learning needs of students at the centre. However, students are among the least well-equipped of the stakeholders to recognise quality. It is very easy to confuse satisfaction for quality, since students may enjoy careers lessons or interviews without knowing how much better they might have been.

Stakeholders have their own legitimate concerns and requirements of a quality assurance scheme. The government, for example, as a principal stakeholder in CEG, is particularly interested in the contribution of CEG to economic regeneration. CEG will help to motivate students to acquire higher skill levels in areas crucial to the country's success in global markets. Employers have an interest in ensuring that CEG focuses on equipping young people with the skills needed for employability. Ideally, the criteria used to measure quality should focus on the needs of students. In practice, schemes are likely to reflect the areas of common agreement between the principal stakeholders and are better for having been drawn up following extensive consultation between all those involved.

The key elements and characteristics of high-quality careers education and guidance identified in *Looking Forward* (SCAA, 1995) are:

A coherent teaching programme
There should be a planned and coordinated programme of courses and activities within the curriculum for all pupils. The programme should be relevant and appropriate to the ages and abilities of pupils and an agreed amount of time allocated to it. It should be designed to prepare pupils for the opportunities, responsibilities and experiences of working life.

Continuing guidance
Support for pupils should be continuing, with additional help when pupils enter and leave school and when they choose their options. Careers guidance should be an integral part of the school's overall approach to pastoral care and clearly linked to the other components of careers education and guidance. The roles and responsibilities of formal providers of guidance, in particular the Careers Service and teachers, need to be clearly recognised. Careers guidance must be impartial, confidential and based on the needs of the individual.

Accurate information
Comprehensive, reliable and up-to-date information should be provided for pupils of all ages and abilities. Material should be well displayed and maintained with ease of access. Information should include a range of printed, audio-visual and IT-based materials. Pupils should be given opportunities to acquire the skills they need to make the best use of information.

Experience of work
A wide variety of experiences of the working world should be provided as part of the curriculum. The school should work closely with business and other parties to offer a range of suitable learning activities.

Action planning and the recording of achievement
Action planning in which pupils consider the appropriate next steps while at school, helps them to make better choices and decisions. The recording of achievement encourages pupils to keep a systematic record of their personal successes in and out of school.

The Role of Inspection

The establishment of new arrangements for the inspection of schools and colleges has also prompted considerable interest in the scope for inspecting careers education and guidance as a method of checking quality and standards. In the first two years of secondary school inspections by the Office for Standards in Education (OFSTED), many careers teachers have expressed their frustration at the shortcomings of the Framework for Inspection to provide them with detailed evaluative judgements about quality and standards in this area of the curriculum, for which they are responsible.

In part, the problem reflects the shortage of inspectors nationally who are sufficiently knowledgeable about careers education and guidance to make judgements about it; but it also reflects the difficulty of providing an in-depth inspection of careers education and guidance in the context of a whole-school inspection. In *Competitiveness: Forging Ahead* (DTI, 1995), the government announced its intention to strengthen the OFSTED Framework for Inspection to ensure that inspectors seek evidence that schools have provided good careers education and impartial guidance. This may still not be enough to satisfy careers teachers; but it should provide a firmer foundation for carrying out national surveys on the state of provision. Another announcement, in *Forging Ahead,* which should help with this is the new commitment to improving the links between OFSTED, the Further Education Inspectorate and the quality assurance operation for the Careers Service. Closer links between these agencies will focus attention on continuity and progression in careers education and guidance for students and greater clarity in the roles and responsibilities of schools, colleges and Careers Services in this field.

CHAPTER 17

IMPROVING PROFESSIONAL PRACTICE THROUGH EVALUATION

David Frost

It is unfortunate that evaluation has become such a specialist activity that ordinary practitioners often lack the skills or at least the confidence to undertake it. The situation is somewhat analogous to the house-buying system, which Michael Joseph railed against in his popular book, *The Conveyancing Fraud*. Joseph's mission in life was to encourage us all to do away with the services of solicitors and do our own conveyancing. His message was simply this: it's easy; anybody can do it; just use your common sense and get on with it. I want to argue here that it is time for careers practitioners to take steps to wrest evaluation from the grasp of the professional evaluators and, instead, embrace it as a tool for improvement and change. Of course, there may always be some demand for professional evaluators but, at the present time, I would argue that a great deal of the funding spent on evaluation contracts could be put to better use by channelling it directly into the development of professional practice.

Demystifying Evaluation

First, we need to become more assertive and confident so that we are not so easily put off by the highly technical approach and the esoteric jargon of those who want to corner the market in evaluation. Even some of the experts themselves concede that evaluation needs to be demystified. David Hopkins, for example, prefaces his extremely useful book, *Evaluation for School Improvement*, with a rather apt quotation from Lawrence Stenhouse:

> 'I think... there is some danger that evaluators create their own establishment and glamourise it as an elite. Let's keep hold of the idea that it is mostly a matter of common sense and learning from experience. That is not entirely true but it keeps us from going technical or theological; and a little modest

over-simplification is better than a lapse into jargon or pretentiousness.'
(Stenhouse in Hopkins, 1989)

What is the Purpose of Evaluation?

Some might assume, of course, that the purpose of evaluation is to provide evidence to enable those who make decisions about funding, to judge whether or not the money has been well spent but, as professionals, we need to think through for ourselves the proper relationship between evaluation and the development of professional practice. What part can evaluation play in:

- an individual's professional development?
- curriculum development?
- organisational development?

Evaluation sponsored by outsiders has tended to be of limited value in changing practice. What I propose here instead, is a model based on what has been called a 'collegial' approach to evaluation, which rests on the notion of 'collaborative enquiry, based on shared understanding and knowledge' (Nixon, 1992, p.21).

A Collegial Model of Evaluation

The essential feature of the collegial approach is that the people who are directly involved in the development itself, are also the people who undertake the evaluation – they collaborate to evaluate their own practice, in order to improve that practice. This accords with the view put forward by Lawrence Stenhouse when he said that 'evaluation should... lead development and be integrated with it. Then the conceptual distinction between development and evaluation is destroyed and the two merge as research' (Stenhouse 1975, p.122).

Stenhouse's work led to the blossoming of what has since become widely known as, 'action research' and it is this tradition which I believe holds most promise for careers education and guidance practitioners today.

Action Research and Professional Practice

So, what is action research? It is a way of integrating development and evaluation which puts practitioners at the heart of the process. According to Professor John Elliott: 'The fundamental aim of action research is to improve practice rather than produce knowledge. The production and utilisation of knowledge is subordinate to and conditioned by, this fundamental aim' (Elliott, 1991, p.49).

This is not to say of course that Elliott or anyone else writing about action research would say that the generation of knowledge is unimportant. The point is that it is the practitioner who becomes knowledgeable and is therefore able to improve practice.

Distinguishing Features of Action Research

A recent book by Altricher, Posch and Somekh (1993), *Teachers Investigate Their Work*, provides a very practical and comprehensive account of action research methodology and I have borrowed heavily from it to summarise the distinguishing features of the approach.

1. *Action research is conducted by those directly concerned.* As I hope I have made clear above, action research essentially means practitioner research.
2. *Action research may be facilitated by outsiders.* Action research may arise out of an individual's or an institutional concern. Local authority advisers, higher education tutors and other consultants may be bought in to provide support and guidance and, more unusually, an external agency may initiate an action research project. Whatever the source of the initiative, it would always be the case that the *researchers* are the practitioners.
3. *Action research is concerned with practical problem solving and improvement in practice.* As John Elliott's definition above suggests, the point of action research is to improve practice rather than to add to the sum of knowledge about a particular topic. Of course, it might be said that all research is ultimately aimed at practical concerns but, within the action research framework, there is a direct and continuous relationship.
4. *Action research is values driven.* This is to say that the starting point for action research is the subjective perception that there is an issue. It may be that there is a gap between the practitioner's aims and what is happening in practice; it may be that there is a simple conviction that there is room for improvement. Action researchers do not waste time trying to achieve the questionable goal of objectivity, but are rigorous about declaring their value positions and how these determine their perceptions of the issues.
5. *Action researchers use common sense enquiry strategies.* For some the word 'research' conjures up an image of white-coated scientists using sophisticated data-gathering instruments and complicated formulas for statistical analysis. This is an unhelpful stereotype which tends to undermine the confidence of the practitioner researcher who needs to adopt methods which can easily be integrated into everyday professional practice.
6. *Action research involves both 'reflection in action' and 'reflection on action'.* We are indebted to Donald Schon whose seminal book *The Reflective Practitioner* provides a remarkable, theoretical account of the way in which professional practitioners cultivate and use professional knowledge. Schon's distinction helps us to think about how, within action research, we can become more aware of and record the judgements we make while 'thinking on our feet' (Schon, 1983).

7. *Action research takes a variety of forms.* Although there are many models offered in the literature on action research, its great strength is that it is being constantly renewed and reborn. The networking process leads to a sharing of ideas about enquiry strategies and a great diversity of approaches.

8. *The fruits of action research are made public in the form of case studies.* In his presidential address to the British Educational Research Association in 1979, Lawrence Stenhouse gave us a liberating definition of research, when he said that research is 'systematic enquiry made public' (Stenhouse, 1980). The publication aspect is essential if practice is to be open to scrutiny, although 'publication' does not have to be in the form of journal articles or items in books. To publish may be simply to produce a report to an appropriate audience, such as a committee within a school. I will consider the matter of case studies in an illustrative way below.

An Externally Funded Action Research Project

What follows is an account of a project that is based on a collegial model, but it is also one which responds to the need for accountability in the context of external funding.

In 1994 Kent Careers and Guidance Service established a project aimed at working with careers teachers and careers officers to develop a year 9/10 curriculum for careers education and they called on their local HEI for support (see Chapter 7). The objective was to pilot a curriculum programme in a dozen schools and redesign it for the local context. The funding, made available by the Department for Employment was channelled through Kent TEC, a categorical funding scenario which, inevitably, demanded some kind of accountability driven approach to evaluation. The curriculum adopted is one which is based on experiential learning principles and so the project leaders were concerned that the participating practitioners would need to develop a considerable degree of ownership of the innovation. Unless the practitioners could fully grasp and develop the principles underpinning the teaching and learning approach, the innovation would be ineffective. Understandably, the project leaders wanted to support a collegial approach to evaluation.

The funding was used to release teachers for a number of days so that they could join with careers officers and a range of external advisers and specialists, in a series of workshops. The first step was to agree on a set of process aims or principles of procedure. Principles of procedure are essentially statements about the values and principles which underpin our common endeavour. We saw these principles as provisional and careers coordinators were encouraged to work with their colleagues to refine them in the light of experience in the classroom. The principles are that:

- careers lessons should enable students to review their prior knowledge of the topic; and,
- students should be enabled to explore a new theme actively by exploring their own experience and contexts familiar to them.

The second task was to agree on a specification of possible quality indicators, so that we had a way of recognising whether or not we were realising the principles in practice. For example, if we take the second of the two principles mentioned above, we might say that quality would be indicated if:

- students are able to recognise the theme;
- students describe experiences which are relevant to the theme;
- students feel that the problem is one which is relevant to their circumstances.

Again, we expected that these indicators would be adjusted by each of the school-based groups in the light of their experience in the classroom.

Finally, we needed to share ideas about the sorts of evidence that could be gathered to support a more systematic analysis of the issues emerging. The specification about evidence gathering was seen not as a common plan, but rather as a menu which school-based teams could choose from. For example, in relation to the second principle mentioned above, we suggested that evidence could be gathered in the following ways.

- The teacher could observe the group discussion and record what the students say.
- A colleague could be asked to observe the lesson, to note the way that students respond and how effective the exploration task is.
- A small group of students could be interviewed after the lesson, to find out whether they felt that the discussion was relevant.

Having worked through all of the principles and indicators in this way we had identified a full menu of evidence gathering-strategies as set out below.

Possible Evidence Gathering Strategies

1. *Observation of lessons by colleagues.* Most people are a bit nervous of being observed and so it is important for the observer and the observed to agree on what will be observed and how feedback will be given.
2. *The teacher's journal or log.* The teacher's own observations and reflections can be recorded during the lesson or immediately afterwards. These notes could be structured in advance or just a matter of whatever appears to be significant or interesting.

3. *Curriculum planning documents.* Being able to look through a carefully compiled collection of syllabus documents and lesson plans is invaluable when trying to identify the issues.

4. *Students' journals.* Students' perceptions can be gathered routinely by asking the class, or perhaps just a small sample of students, to record their thoughts and feelings about the lesson in a notebook. This is probably best structured in advance by providing headings and particular time slots for journal entries to be made.

5. *Interviews with students.* It is best to choose a sample of 'reliable informants' and ask someone (a PGCE student, a classroom assistant, a colleague) to conduct a semi-structured interview. Tell the interviewer what you think the issues might be, but make sure the students have the space to raise their own.

6. *Interviews with teachers.* Again, semi-structured or conversational interviews are best, and the issues can easily be noted down. Make sure that everybody knows the ground rules about who can see the notes and so on.

7. *Other artefacts or remains.* There may be such things as notes on flip charts following a team brainstorming session or a classroom activity. There may be vital evidence here which will inform the evaluation.

8. *Students' written reflections.* Students can be asked to make comments about what they think they have learnt and what they think about the activities and materials used in the lessons, as part of their written follow-up tasks.

9. *The teacher's interpretations of students' work.* Whatever written follow-up tasks there may be, the teacher's annotations and summaries of what students appear to have learned, will help to identify issues in the evaluation.

10. *The proceedings of the team.* This evidence is often overlooked, but it is crucial to a grasp of the issues as they emerged for the teachers involved. It is not just a matter of the perceptions and experiences of the individuals concerned but of the nature of the arguments and the action steps which were decided upon along the way.

It was emphasised from the start that local teams would have to draw up their own evaluation plans using the above specifications as guidance. It was important that the teams planned a process of evaluation which was practical, and fitted into their individual circumstances. They would need to agree firstly on the principles, indicators and evidence required. They would then have to agree how the evidence was to be collected and analysed; how the analysis would be discussed and how action steps would be agreed upon and implemented. It might be supposed that such autonomy could lead to a reduction in the rigour of the evaluation process as a whole, or that the validity of the findings at the school level is questionable. On the contrary, I would argue that the validity and relative weight of findings can be gauged and taken account of, provided that there is a reasonable level of coherence across the project as a whole, and provided that each school-based team has made explicit the nature of the evaluation process as it developed for them, and the particular methods of evaluation adopted. These would be made explicit in the form of a case study.

The required outcome for each school-based group was a case study, which would illuminate the curriculum package in action and would identify issues and ways in which the materials could be improved. Each group was asked to produce a short report and the following planning guide was provided.

Case Study Planner

Use these two pages to help plan your report. Why not make copies and ask your colleagues to note down what they think should be included.

Introduction

Describe here the circumstances; who was involved, which classes, what was the evaluation plan, etc.

Account of evaluation

Describe here how the evaluation actually went, how it changed direction or failed to work according to plan. You should also record the ways in which the classroom practice was adapted in the light of early evaluation.

Summary of evidence

Describe here the evidence you were able to collect, indicate what kind of information you could get from it. Include items of evidence in the appendix.

Analysis

Describe here what you and your colleagues discovered by looking at the evidence. Use the principles as thematic headings, eg 'Reviewing previous knowledge'.

Summary of problems arising

Describe here any issues or problems discovered through the evaluation.

Summary of suggested adaptations

Describe here any suggestions for adapting the materials.

Summary of proposals or principles for teaching

Describe here any suggestions for ways in which to teach this programme.

The case studies from all of the participating schools showed some diversity in terms of the evaluation process adopted, but the approach was similar enough to be able to relate one to the other. The reports identified similar issues and so it was possible to trawl through them and bring together issues and ideas for adapting the materials. It is important to note that within this essentially 'illuminative model' (see Parlett and Hamilton, 1972) we were not interested in proving the effectiveness of the programme, but wanted to reveal the full range of issues and bring together the judgements of experienced practitioners. The case studies together would support some generalisation, but our achievement would be in terms of our collective professional understanding rather than some kind of hard and fast judgement about whether this package was better than another one.

In this project we were able to combine what I portrayed earlier as opposing models, in a way that would lead to the improvement in quality of practice, through participative classroom research, and could also satisfy the fundholders who needed to be assured that their money was being well spent.

The above case is of a large-scale project with a degree of central direction. The school-based teams are facilitated and led by an outside agency which has the ability to drive the innovation because of categorical funding. This does not suggest, however, that collegial evaluation has to be organised in this way by outsiders. Indeed the skills of evaluation are more likely to be developed through small scale initiatives. Set out below, are two typical scenarios where the initiative comes directly from the practitioners concerned.

Small-scale Action Research: Case Study A

A careers adviser working under a service level agreement within a school, ran group sessions with year 12 students from time to time. Her Careers Service manager told all the careers advisers at a monthly team meeting that, in the future, they would be expected to provide many more group sessions than in the past. This individual was concerned, because the group sessions she had run so far had not gone very well: she wondered whether her skills were adequate and whether the division of labour between her and the careers teacher was appropriate. She discussed the problem with colleagues who had similar feelings and they asked one of the development team to provide support to enable them to assess their concerns.

The development officer suggested a programme of action research. They began by meeting to discuss their concerns in more detail and to plan the next action steps. The outcome of the meeting was peer observation arrangement where the careers advisers agreed to pair up and observe each other running a group session. The arrangement included clear rules about feedback and action steps for individual practitioners. At a further meeting the issues and action steps were shared without jeopardising individuals' reputations. A decision was taken that it would be helpful to collaborate with careers coordinators to try to identify principles underpinning good group facilitation. After further classroom experiments and observations, a handbook of guidance for running group sessions was produced and circulated throughout the Careers Service and the schools it served.

Small-scale Action Research: Case Study B

In a comprehensive school, the senior management team received a proposal from the careers coordinator to enhance the year 10 PSE (Personal and Social Education) programme to allow for a series of careers education lessons. The head of RE made strong representations to the senior management team opposing the move because of the resulting reduction in time allocated to religious and moral education. The careers coordinator subsequently secured a small grant from the

School/Business Partnership to pay for additional resources and this gave weight to the proposal. It was agreed that PSE would be given more time in the timetable to allow for the careers input, but it would be on a trial basis for one year and would need to be evaluated and reviewed in the following May.

In the autumn term the careers coordinator approached the head of year 10 to discuss the difficulty. It was agreed that the provision of religious, personal, social and moral education as a whole would be looked at by the tutor team. The head of RE was invited to the meetings and asked to take a leading role in conducting an audit. This exercise led to a decision to gather evidence about the students' perceptions of all these aspects of their curriculum experience. The evaluation exercise opened up a positive dialogue between the head of RE and the careers coordinator. In the following spring, the group agreed on the provision of a more fully integrated PSE programme which included a balance of RE and careers education. The careers coordinator was able to produce a short report for the School/Business Partnership, indicating that the funds provided by them had led to careers education being established in the year 10 curriculum.

Rigour and Accountability

The notion that a collegial approach to evaluation is incompatible with accountability within a categorical funding context, is clearly untenable. A look back at the TVEI experience will tell us that a great many evaluation reports were written only to gather dust in someone's filing cabinet. The Training Agency was obliged to ask for evaluations, but what it really wanted was to maximise the impact of the available funding and to encourage self-evaluation towards that end, but the practitioners did not always have the skills or confidence to carry out credible evaluation.

If we are to derive maximum benefit from the funds now forthcoming from the Department for Education and Employment and elsewhere, we need to make sure that evaluation is an integral part of the project development, rather than a bolt-on exercise carried out by external evaluators. Of course, fundholders will need to be persuaded that the route to cost effectiveness involves enabling practitioners to use evaluation as a strategy for the development of practice. I would suggest, therefore, that careers practitioners need to give urgent consideration not only to the question of how they can develop skills for evaluation, but also to the question of how they can demonstrate to fundholders that evaluation is an essential part of good professional practice.

REFERENCES AND FURTHER READING

ADSET (1995) *The Careers Software Journal*, Association for Database Services in Education and Training (ADSET).

Altricher, H, Posch, P and Somekh, B (1993) *Teachers Investigate Their Work: An introduction to the methods of action research*, London: Routledge.

Andrews, D, Barnes, A and Law, B (1995) *Staff Development for Careers Work*, Cambridge: Careers Research and Advisory Centre (CRAC), Hobsons.

Ashton, DN (1992) 'The Resructuring of the Labour Market and Youth Training', in *Education for Economic Survival,* P Brown and H Lauder (eds), London: Routledge.

Audit Commission/OFSTED (1993) *Unfinished Business, Full-Time Educational Courses for 16–19 Year Olds*, London: HMSO.

Avent, C (1985) *Practical Approaches to Careers Education*, Cambridge: Hobsons.

Ball, C (1991) *Learning Pays*, London: RSA.

Ball, C (1992) *Profitable Learning*, London: RSA.

Barnes, A (1993) *Beyond School: Community and Careers*, London: HMSO.

Barnes, A (1993) *Cross Curricular Theme Pack 5 Careers Education and Guidance*, Pearson.

Barnes, D (1989) 'Knowledge as Action' in *Development in Learning and Assessment*, B Moon and Murphy P (eds), Milton Keynes: OUP.

Bevan, P (1995) 'Using Personal Construct Theory in Careers Education, *NACGT Bulletin*, February 1995, National Association of Careers and Guidance Teachers (NACGT).

Bethel, A (1979) *Eye Openers I*, Cambridge: Cambridge University Press

Birmingham Careers Service (BCS) (1990) *Planning a Student Centred Approach to Careers Education*, Birmingham: BCS.

Bradshaw, D (ed.) (1995) *Bringing Learning to Life*, Lewes: Falmer Press.

British Film Institute (BFI) (1991) *Secondary Media Education: A Curriculum Statement*, London: BFI.

CBI (1989) *Towards a Skills Revolution*, London: Confederation of British Industry (CBI)

CBI (1993a) *Routes for Success*, London: CBI.

CBI (1993b) *A Credit to Your Career*, London: CBI.

Cleaton, D (1993) *Survey of Careers Work*, Institute of Careers Guidance (ICG)/NACGT.

CRAC (1989) Computers in Guidance, Conference Report 1989, Careers Research and Advisory Centre.

Dearing, R (1994) *The National Curriculum and its Assessment*, London: SCAA.

DES and DE (1991) *Education and Training for the 21st Century*, Volume 1, London: HMSO.

DES/HMI (1988) *Curriculum Matters 10: Careers Education and Guidance from 5 to 16*, London: HMSO.

DES, DE and Welsh Office (1987) *Working Together for a Better Future*, London: Central Office of Information.

DES (1972) *Teacher Education – Report of the committee of inquiry under the Chairmanship of Lord James of Rusholme*, London: HMSO.

DES (1978) *Making INSET Work – In-service Education and Training for Teachers: A basis for discussion*, London: DES.

DES (1992) HMI *Survey of Guidance 13–19 in Schools and Sixth Form Colleges*, London: DES.

DES (1988) *Education Reform Act*, London: HMSO.

DfE (1993) *Education Act*, London: DfE.

DfE/ED (1994) *Better Choices, Working Together to Improve Careers Education and Guidance – The Principles*, London: DfE/ED,

DfE (1994) *Circular 14/94*, London: DfE.

Dryden, W and Watts, AG (1993) *Guidance and Counselling in Britian: a 20 year perspective*, Cambridge: CRAC.

DTI (1994) *Competitiveness: Helping Business to Win*, London: HMSO.

DTI (1995) *Competiveness: Forging Ahead*, London: HMSO.

DE (1982) *Vocational Guidance Interviews*, A survey by the Careers Service Inspectorate, London: DE.

ED (1993a) *Assessing the Effects of First Phase Training Credits*, Sheffield: ED.

ED (1993b) *Requirements and Guidance for Providers*, Sheffield: ED.

ED/DfE (1994) *Better Choices – The Principles*, London: ED/DfE.

ED/DfE (1995) *Better Choices – From Principles into Practice*, London: ED/DfE.

Edwards, A and Talbot, R (1994) *The Hard-pressed Researcher: A research handbook for the caring professions*, London: Longman.

Edwards, AJ (ed.) (1994) *Career Guides*, Network Education Press/Kent County Council.

Elliott, J (1991) *Action Research for Educational Change*, Milton Keynes: OUP.

FEFC/OFSTED (1994) *16–19 Guidance*, Coventry: FEFC.

Finegold, D (1992) 'Economic Changes Driving Education Reform' in *Work Related Teaching and Learning in Schools*, W Richardson (ed.), Unpublished paper, University of Warwick.

Frost, D (1995) Integrating Systematic Enquiry into Everyday Professsional Practice: Towards some principles of procedure, *British Educational Research Journal Vol 21, No 3*.

Frost, D (1995a) in *Teacher Education: Some issues from research and practice*, R McBride (ed), Lewes: Falmer Press.

Fullan, M (1993) *Change Forces*, Lewes: Falmer Press.

Graham, D and Tytler D (1992) *Lesson for Us All: Making of the National Curriculum*, London: Routledge.

Harland, J, Kinder, K and Keys, W (1993) *Restructuring INSET: Privatisation and its alternatives*, Slough: NFER.

Hawthorn, R (1995) *First Steps: Quality standards for guidance across all sectors*, London: RSA.

HMI (1973) *Careers Education in Secondary Schools, Education Survey 18*, London: HMSO.

HMI (1992) *Survey of Guidance 13–19 in Schools and Sixth Form Colleges*, London: DES.

Hopkins, D (1989) *Evaluation for School Improvement*, Milton Keynes: OUP.

Hutton, W (1995) *The State We're In*, London: Jonathan Cape.

Jones, A (1990) 'New Policy Directions' in *Guidance and Educational Change: Cross-sectoral review of policy and practice*, AG Watts (ed), Cambridge: CRAC.

Joseph, M (1976) *The Conveyancing Fraud*, London: Michael Joseph.

Justice, C (1991) *On Target*, London: Brent Careers Service.

KCGS (Kent Careers and Guidance Service) (1994) *Supporting Careers Work*, Maidstone: KCGS.

Killeen, J, and Kidd, J (1993) *Learning Outcomes of Guidance: A Review of Recent Research, Employment Department Research Paper No 85*, London: ED.

Killeen, J, White, M and Watts, AG (1992) *The Economic Value of Careers Guidance*, London: Policy Studies Institute.

Law, B *et al* (1991b) *Coordinating Careers Work*, Sheffield: COIC.

Law, B, Andrews, D and Barnes, A (1995b) *Making Careers Work*, Cambridge: CRAC.

Law, B (1993) *Teachers Business – Careers Education and Guidance*, Oxford: Teacher Placement Service.

Law, B and Watts, AG (1977) *Schools, Careers and Community*, London: Church Information Centre.

Law, B *et al* (1991a) (Revised 1995a) *Careers Work*, Manchester: Open College.

McNiff, J (1988) *Action Research: Principles and Practices*, London: MacMillan.

Morris, M and Stoney, S (1995) *The Role of the Careers Service in Careers Education and Guidance in Schools*.

Murphy, R and Torrance, H (eds) (1987) *Evaluating Education: Issues and Methods*, London: Paul Chapman.

NCC (1990) *Curriculum Guidance 6: Careers Education and Guidance*, York: NCC.

National Commission on Education (1994) *Learning to Succeed – A Radical Look at Education Today and a Strategy for the Future*, London: Paul Hamlyn Foundation.

NCET (1992) *Careers Software Training Pack*, Warwick: NCET.

NCET (1993) *Using Software Menus in Careers Education and Guidance*, Warwick: NCET.

NCET (1994) *Computer-Assisted Guidance: Using IT to provide careers and educational guidance*, Warwick: NCET.

NCET (1995) *Getting Involved in Careers Work* (Interactive video), Warwick: NCET.

NCET, CRAC and NICEC (1994) *The Future Use of Information Technology in Guidance*, Warwick: NCET, CRAC and NICEC.

NCVQ (1992) *Action Planning and the National Record of Achievement*, NCVQ.

Nixon, J (1992) *Evaluating the Whole Curriculum*, Milton Keynes: OUP.

Parlett, M and Hamilton, D (1972) 'Evaluation and Illumination: a new approach to the study of innovative programmes' in *Beyond the Numbers Game*, D Hamilton et al (eds), London: MacMillan.

Raffe, D (1992) *Participation of 16–18 Year Olds in Education and Training*, National Commission on Education.

Rudduck, J (1988) 'The Ownership of Change as a Basis for Teacher's Professional Learning' in *Teachers Professional Learning*, J Calderhead (ed), Lewes: Falmer Press.

Rudduck, J (1991) *Innovation and Change*, Milton Keynes: OUP.

SCAA (1995) *Looking Forward*, London: SCAA.

Schon, D (1983) *The Reflective Practitioner – How Professionals Think in Action*, London: Avebury.

Spours, K (1992) *Recent Developments in Qualifications at 14+: A Critical Review Working Paper No 12*, University of London: Institute of Education.

Squirrel, G (1994) *Individual Action Planning: A practical guide*, London: David Fulton.

Stenhouse, L (1975) *Introduction to Curriculum Research and Development*, London: Heineman.

Stenhouse, L (1980) 'The Study of Samples and the Study of Cases', *British Educational Research Journal, Vol 6 No 1*.

Swanson, G (1991) 'Representation' in *Media Study Book: A guide for teachers*, D Lusted (ed.), London: Routledge.

Trades Union Congress (1991) *Skills 2000*, London: TUC.

Universum Verlagsanstalt (1992) *New tendencies, challenges and technologies in transnational careers guidance* (Third European conference on computers in careers guidance, Nuremberg) Wiesbaden: Universum Verlagsans-talt.

Waterhouse, P (1988) *Supported Self-Study: An Introduction for Teachers*, NCET.

Watts, AG (1986) 'The Careers Service and Schools: A changing relationship', *British Journal of Guidance and Counselling*, Vol 14, No2, pp 168–86.

Watts, AG, (1991) 'The Impact of the "New Right": Policy challenges confronting Careers Guidance in England and Wales', *British Journal of Guidance and Counselling, Vol 19, No 3*.

Watts, AG, (1993) *Promoting Careers: Guidance for Learning and Work, National Commission on Education, Briefing No 15*.

Watts, AG (1995) 'Applying market principles to the delivery of careers guidance services', *British Journal of Guidance and Counselling, Vol 23, No 1, pp 69–81*.

Wellington, J (1993) *The Work-Related Curriculum*, London: Kogan Page.

Westergaard, J and Barnes, A (1994) *Inspecting Careers Work*, Chelmsford: TVEI.

Whitehead, M (1989) 'Reading – Caught or Taught?' in *Development in Learning and Assessment* Moon, B and Murphy, P (eds) Milton Keynes: OUP.

Whiteside, T (1994) 'Tutoring and guidance post-16: the student's view', *The Curriculum Journal, Vol 5, No 3*.

Whitty, G, Rowe, G and Aggleton, P (1994) 'Subjects and Themes in the Secondary School Curriculum', *Research Papers in Education, Vol 9, No 2, pp 159–81*.

Wood, D (1988) *How Children Think and Learn*, Oxford: Blackwell.

Wyatt, J (1993) 'Portfolio Development in INSET: Using the Open Learning Materials with Careers Teachers', *NICEC Careers Education and Guidance Bulletin, No 41, 1993*, NICEC.

GLOSSARY

ADSET	Association for Database Services in Education and Training
CAGS	computer-assisted guidance systems
CA	careers adviser
CBI	Confederation of British Industry
CASCAID	Careers Advisory Service Computer Aid
CEG	careers education and guidance
CID	careers information database
CO	careers officer
CRAC	Careers Research and Advisory Centre
DE	Department of Employment
DES	Department of Education and Science (now DfEE)
DfE	Department for Education (now DfEE)
DfEE	Department for Education and Employment
DOTS	Decision making skills: Opportunity awareness: Transition learning: Self-awareness
DTI	Department of Trade and Industry
EBD	educational and behavioural difficulties
EBP	education–business partnership
ED	Employment Department
FEFC	Further Education Funding Council
GEST	Grant for Education Support and Training
GNVQ	General National Vocational Qualification
GRIST	Grant-Related In-service Training
HE	higher education
HEI	higher education institution
HMI	Her Majesty's Inspectors
HMSO	Her Majesty's Stationery Office
IAP	individual action plan
ICG	Institute of Careers Guidance
INSET	in-service training
ISCO	Independent Schools Careers Organisation

IT	information technology
ITT	initial teacher training
JIIG-CAL	Job Ideas and Information Generator, Computer-assisted Learning
KCGS	Kent Careers and Guidance Service
LEA	Local Education Authority
LEATGS	Local Education Authority Training Grants Scheme
LMI	Labour Market Information
MLD	moderate learning difficulties
NACGT	National Association of Careers and Guidance Teachers
NCC	National Curriculum Council (now replaced by SCAA)
NFER	National Foundation for Education Research
NICEC	National Institute for Careers Education and Counselling
NCET	National Council for Educational Technology
NRA	National Record of Achievement
NTET	National Targets for Education and Training
NVQ	National Vocational Qualification
OFSTED	Office for Standards in Education
PETRA	European Community Action Programme for the Vocational Training of Young People and their Preparation for Adult and Working Life.
PGCE	postgraduate certificate in education
PSHE	personal, social and health education
PSE	personal and social education
RoA	Record of Achievement
SEN	special education and needs
SENCO	Special Educational Needs Coordinator
SCAA	School Curriculum and Assessment Authority
SCIP	School Curriculum Industry Partnership
SLD	severe learning difficulties
TEC	Training and Enterprise Council
TEED	Training, Enterprise and Education Directorate (of the Employment Department)
TPS	Teacher Placement Service
TTA	Teacher Training Agency
TVEI(E)	Technical and Vocational Education Initiative (and Extension)
UCAS	Universities and Colleges Admissions System

INDEX

accreditation 100
action planning 29, 97, 121
   and recording of achievement 144
   in careers education and guidance
     programmes 29–32
   whole institution approach 31
   with special needs students 33–4
action research
   case study examples 154–5
   case study planner 152–3
   collegial model 149
   distinguishing features 148–9
   evidence gathering strategies 150–51
Advanced Certificate in Careers Education
   and Guidance 114
Associate Tutors 106–8

Canterbury, Christ Church College 105,
   133, 136
careers advisers
   role in computer-assisted guidance 71
   role in Education for Choice project
     63
Careers Service 7, 10, 15–18, 24, 140, 145
   requirement for guidance providers 8
   service level agreements 10, 23
'Careers Work' 105, 106
change 119
   management of 122, 123
   virtuous circle for 86
Commission for Racial Equality Code of
   Practice 21
community-linked work 87, 116
competence and training 88

competitive tendering 7
computer-assisted guidance
   and key issues about CEG 70
   and learning systems 70
   matching people to opportunities 68
   to supplement human guidance 71
Confederation of British Industry (CBI)
   6, 11
   A Credit to Your Career 7
   careership 6–7
   guidance vouchers 7
   Routes for Success 7
consultation with senior managers 102
coordination, of careers education 88
core skills 20
courses, staff development 87, 89, 93
cross-curricular work 87, 115
curriculum development, a
     teacher-researcher model 60

Department for Education and
     Employment 155
Department for Education 8, 10
   Consultation Paper 10
Department of Trade and Industry (DTI)
     White Papers
   Forging Ahead 10, 21, 140, 145
   Helping Business to Win 9
development planning 95, 104
   'bottom-up' 100
development priorities 95
differentialist and developmentalist
     approaches to guidance 14
DOTS model 115

East Sussex 114, 131
economic benefits of careers education
   132
Education Act 1993 21
'Education for Choice'
   evaluation issues 62–3
   implementation in France 57–9
   objectives of project 62–3
   stages of programme 56–7
   relevance in UK 59
Education Reform Act 1988
Employment Department 8, 9, 10, 149
   Better Choices booklets 10, 21, 25–6
   careers information initiative 8, 140
   Year 9 and 10 initiative 9, 149
enquiry and development 94, 98
   strategies 99
entitlement to CEG 9–10
evaluation 146–155
   collegial approach 147
   in action research 148–155
   managing change through 122
   of guidance practice 15
experiential learning
   in special needs programmes 52
   role in delivery of CEG 56

Further Education Funding Council
   (FEFC) 122
Further Education Inspectorate 145

General National Vocational Qualification
   (GNVQ) 101
Grants for Education Support and
   Training (GEST) 93, 140
guidance
   and support 87
   economic cost of 36
   tutorial role in 38–9
guidance vouchers 8

initial teacher training (ITT) 85
Inservice Training for Teachers
   (INSET) 93
Inspectors 10
Investors in People (IIP) 141

Kent Careers and Guidance Service 105

joint training of careers teachers and
   careers advisers 111

local authorities 105, 106

managing careers work 87
motivation
   improving student motivation 28
   in Education for Choice project 60

National Curriculum
   attainment targets 8
   cross-curricular themes 8
   Dearing Review 9, 21
National Curriculum Council 11
National Foundation for Education
      Research (NFER) 17
National Institute for Careers Education
      and Counselling (NICEC) 10
National Targets for Education and
      Training (NTETs) 140–41
new vocational pathways post-14 9

occupational structures 12
Office for Standards in Education
      (OFSTED) 10, 120, 126, 145
   Framework of Inspection 21, 145
Open College 98, 109
opportunity structures 15
Oxted County School 114

parents
   response to Education for Choice
      project 64
   views considered in action planning
      activity 33
Parents Charter 21
personal development plan 95
Personal and Social and Health Education
      (PSHE) 85
portfolio
   development 90, 94, 99, 101
   use in Education for Choice project 62
post-16 context 122

qualified staff 124
quality and standards 25–6, 140–45
   fitness for purpose 143

Investors in Careers 140
Investors in People (IIP) 140
quasi-markets principles in guidance
    delivery 7, 8

resource centre 87
reporting, recording and reviewing 87,
    117

school
    appointment of careers coordinators
        23–5
    development plan for CEG 23
    governors 19
    managers 19
    policy on CEG 22–3
School Curriculum and Assessment
    Authority (SCAA)
    Looking Forward 21, 144
Service Level Agreement 110
Seychelles 131–7
Special Educational Needs Coordinator
    (SENCO) 116
special educational needs 116
    and examples of delivery in CEG
        33, 34, 53
    and self-awareness 51
    importance of experiential learning 52
staff development 84, 95
    open learning in 89
    reflection in 101, 102
    review in 100
    theory in 88, 119
    tutors in 106–7

Staffordshire Careers Service 109, 114
supported self-study
    definition 39
    management issues in 47
    preparation for 46
    role of materials 41
    stages 39

target setting
    integral to teaching and learning 28
    tutor, role in 117
Teacher Training Agency (TTA) 93
Technical and Vocational Education
    Initiative (TVEI) 8, 21, 116, 140,
    155
theory, *see* staff development
training
    careers advisers and careers coordinators
        18
    NVQ structure 18
Training Credits 7, 8
    see also Youth Credits
Training and Enterprise Councils (TECs)
    8, 140
tutors
    response to Education for Choice
        project 64
    role in guidance process 38

work experience 9
Working Together for a Better Future 9

Youth Credits (formerly Training
    Credits) 8, 140